sacred spaces   *princeton parties, gatherings and celebrations*

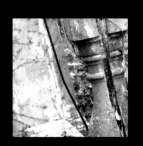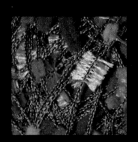

sacred spaces *princeton parties, gatherings and celebrations*

BY debbie tunnell,

dale engelbert and susan szymanski

WITH PHOTOGRAPHY BY ricardo barros

TO DOUG,
FOR HIS UNCONDITIONAL SUPPORT
OF THREE AUTHORS WITH A DREAM.

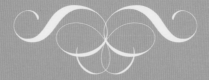

SACRED SPACES
PRINCETON PARTIES, GATHERINGS AND CELEBRATIONS

LIBRARY OF CONGRESS CONTROL NUMBER: 2004094267

ISBN 0-9755997-0-4

PRINTED IN THE UNITED STATES OF AMERICA

BOOK DESIGN BY
SUSAN SZYMANSKI AND DALE ENGELBERT

RECIPEAS 4 U

WWW.RECIPEAS4U.COM

a happy accident

Our recipe for this book project required a commitment of almost three years, a combination of skills, and a lot of long-term patience from every personality involved. But it was the blending of the goals and talents of many individuals whose paths had occasionally crossed that resulted in what Dale called "a happy accident" back in October 2003—quite by accident, the plan to self-publish a book had taken shape. Dale, Susan, and I started this journey in February 2001 as an enthusiastic trio of Princeton moms who enjoyed working together, but we ended it with a long list of fellow creative souls committed to its success. While my original idea was simply to write an entertaining cookbook, over the course of our parties, gatherings, and celebrations, the concept developed into something much more: reflective of the inner workings of my very talented friends Dale Engelbert, Susan Szymanski, Ricardo Barros, Ann Bartholomay, and Ed Batejan. No matter what I asked of them—and I have been known to ask a lot of myself and my friends—each one of these professionals rose to the occasion and helped fulfill my mind's-eye vision.

The attempt to capture the creative cycles of many lives and the capacity of each individual to represent his or her ideas within a space—whether it was internal, external, or based on a memory from the past—could come to fruition only through a dedicated group effort. My talents lie in the kitchen and in concepts and sometimes crazy ideas. I work hard to make sure that what I offer my guests represents what is within my heart. Friends respect this talent, as do I their gifts of technology; their use of color, art, design; their eye for capturing the spirit through a camera lens; or in their creation of sweet representations of friendship through the use of eggs, butter, and flour.

To Ricardo Barros whose flexibility, generosity, and gifted eye captured the essence of each sacred space, we are grateful for your friendship, professionalism, and sense of humor.

To Ed Batejan, who worked tirelessly with us through eight book parties, helping create recipes to set the stage for wonderful gatherings: You are a dear friend whose talents in the kitchen never cease to amaze. Sweet thanks to Annie B, aka Ann Bartholmay, for sharing an enthusiasm for this project, along with your baking skills and talented staff. The endings you imagined for each event always included the right touch of elegance, whimsy, or chocolate.

Our gratitude to Marek Bulaj for his professional flexibility and friendly willingness to join our creative group and for the exquisite photos he produced.

Jack Morrison of Nassau Street Seafood helped us feed hundreds on a shoestring budget. He loaned us his talented chef, Ed Batejan, his well-trained service staff, and his professional catering kitchen for over two years of prime-time events. Dick and Donna Gasior of Gasior's Furniture completed our table setting at Drumthwacket with their exquisite dining chairs. Ellen Yazujian of Ashton Whyte, Wendy Kvalheim of Mottahedeh, and Alyssa Bronstein of the Winged Pig generously offered us the pick of their decorative inventories for our photographs.

To Claudia Himes of Special Occasions and Queens Street Linens in Lancaster, Pennsylvania, our appreciation for selecting beautiful linens for every occasion. John Giammearse and Eric Roberts of Jardinière Florals created arrangements that surprised even the gardeners among us.

Mary Harrison—a lover of paper, gardens, and parties and owner of the wedding and event planning company Euphorbia in Lawrenceville—has an exquisite eye for the perfect paper, china, chair, glass, or lighting. Thank you, Mary, for introducing us to Susan Szymanski of Moonlight Design, who transformed our ideas for invitations and menus into works of art.

Thanks to all the chefs who let me pick their cooking brains and helped me get to the culinary place I wanted to go with a particular recipe or idea: Executive Chef Brian Dougherty of the Blue Point Grill, Chef Choi of Nassau Bagel and Sushi, and José Lopez of Nassau Street Seafood.

Thanks to Maureen Smythe of the Princeton Historical Society for her assistance in researching the history of local families and the properties of Princeton past, and to Laurel Masten Cantor of the Communications Department at Princeton University, who always had a quick answer about usage rights. We would also like to thank Chris Kitto, Meg Rich, Charles Greene, and Ben Primer of the Princeton University Library, Department of Rare Books and Special Collections, for their assistance in obtaining permission to reprint images from the papers of Moses Taylor Pyne and Beatrix Farrand.

We are grateful to Virginia France of the Princeton University Bookstore, Margaret Griffin of Micawber Books, and Nancy

Nichols of the Princeton Barnes and Noble, who offered friendly guidance on how to approach independent publishing. We would like to thank David Joachim and Tom Collins for their initial guidance of this project, and Elizabeth Hague Sword, who helped us find our way through the publishing world. To Dan Halpern of Harper Collins, who put us in contact with our editor, we are forever in your debt.

David Porat of Chelsea Market Baskets in New York City answered our last-minute call and donated his time and products to the Breast Health Center fund-raiser. Peter Zakia of Hopewell House Liquors always managed to find an excellent wine or champagne to please our guests and fit our budget. Cathy Martz and Cindy Smith, our favorite professional party servers, earned our respect and affection by keeping our guests happy and well fed. To each guest who attended one of our parties we appreciate your interest in our book.

Special kudos to Susan's gifted mother, Veronica Szymanski, for stitching more than a hundred Pins and Needles invitations and adding a vintage button to each for that special touch. To all the friends who had enough faith in us to loan us their antique silver, vintage crystal, hand-painted glassware and pottery, a huge thank-you—Amy Clark, Cynthia Hillas, Debbie Lane, Cathy Loevner, Karen Lomax, Ann Mann, and Julie Rauch.

Thank you to Doria Lenicky and Kelly Livesey of Annie B's Confections for translating our ideas into incredible hand-painted cookies, marzipan-wrapped cakes, and buzzing lemon tarts.

Special appreciation goes to Daphne Townsend, Lisa Paine, and Beverly Mills for guiding us through the archives of the Drumthwacket Foundation, and for opening the doors of the Governor's Mansion to us during the summer and fall of 2001, sharing stories about Agnes Taylor Pyne Davis and the restoration of the mansion and gardens.

Thank you to pianist Laurie Altman, cellist Sara Wolfe, koto player Masayo Ishigure, Yuriy Prilutskiy, Michael Huse, and Kurt Engelbert III, and members of the New Jersey Symphony Orchestra for their enchanting music. Thank you to Brian Richardson of L&A Tents for keeping us covered, sometimes at the last minute, and to Karen Graves of Plant Profiles for providing spring and summer plants that added a twinkle to our corners.

To recipe tester Jessica Thomson, who helped me translate sometimes unwritten recipes into text, I offer my gratitude for your enthusiasm and professionalism. Thank you, Kathy Gunst, my IACP mentor, for introducing me to Jessica and answering my beginner's questions. A special appreciation to my niece, Kristy Maguire, for her computer talents and for providing a diversion with my sweet grand-nieces, Princesses Emma and Julia.

To E. Beth Thomas, my editor, second set of eyes, and the trusted lady with the red pencil—your words of encouragement supported me through the final chapter.

A special thanks to each of our family members— Doug, Christopher, Travis, Kurt, Kurt III, Lauren, Keith, Ken, and Jim, who gave us the time and space needed to pull this project together, eating takeout far too often or surviving occasionally on Annie B desserts but not complaining too loudly—our love and appreciation for the three-year gift of time. When you remember us to our great-grandchildren and talk about our crazy "book days," may you also remember the gatherings we created and our hopes and dreams for this project.

A special thanks to Ruth West, our guardian angel.

And finally, to all the neighbors and friends who graciously opened their sacred spaces to us: Fay Sciarra, Shelley Roe, Ann Battle, Marci Kahn, Sunny Haralson, Cynthia and Rob Hillas, Kathleen Gittleman and Rachel Herr, Elizabeth Sword, Janet and Jim Hester, Melita Wright, Anne Reeves, and Liz and Zaki Hosny. Your spaces inspired us to look beyond ourselves and reach to accomplish the forgotten dream living within each of us.

Debbie, Dale, and Susan

wisteria blossoms

I see them on my trellises and walls
And straight way dream of distant waterfalls;
But when to distant waterfalls I roam
I dream of my wisterias at home.

— CHARLES DALMON

contents

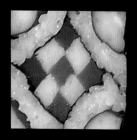

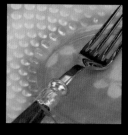

caring people, just like the endless number of other communities that form our nation and our world. We set out to capture that sentiment and understanding in each of our stories about our neighbors and their sacred spaces.

Meaningful spaces are created over time—just ask my mother. Now requiring assistance, she has established her home in a small room filled with photographs, a collection of teapots and chiming clocks, and her beloved Gladys Tabor books. She travels emotionally through time when she sees the people and things that she loves.

Collections become valuable because they capture the essence of who we are. As children, we're able to do this almost instantly with baseball cards or dolls; in adulthood, it seems to take longer to find our niche. Maybe we forget, over time, how important it is to set aside a place, an idea, or a passion that is just about us. Somehow, as we grow older, we realize that it's acceptable to fill a space with 1940s table linens, a blue-painted tree filled with birdhouses, chocolate molds, or hooked rugs. These tokens—while sometimes difficult to explain—also help to make us interesting and unique.

While Princeton is full of extraordinary locations in private, historical, and natural settings, each space we have included has characteristics symbolic of the group, individual, or philosophy featured. We wanted these very personal qualities and identifiable messages to become the true focal point of what we describe as a party, gathering, or celebration. Winter, spring, summer, and fall, we hope you create your own space to enjoy moments with family and friends that are meaningful, beautiful, and most important of all—unforgettable.

Join us as we share *Sacred Spaces, Princeton Parties, Gatherings and Celebrations.*

Debbie, Dale, and Susan

September 2004

the enduring

IF THE AUTUMN ENDED
ERE THE BIRDS FLEW SOUTHWARD,
IF IN THE COLD WITH WEARY THROATS
THEY VAINLY STROVE TO SING,
WINTER WOULD BE ETERNAL;
LEAF AND BUSH AND BLOSSOM
WOULD NEVER ONCE MORE RIOT
IN THE SPRING.

IF REMEMBRANCE ENDED
WHEN LIFE AND LOVE ARE GATHERED,
IF THE WORLD WERE NOT LIVING
LONG AFTER ONE IS GONE,
SONG WOULD NOT RING, NOR SORROW
STAND AT THE DOOR IN EVENING;
LIFE WOULD VANISH AND SLACKEN,
MEN WOULD BE CHANGED TO STONE.

BUT THERE WILL BE AUTUMN'S BOUNTY
DROPPING UPON OUR WEARINESS,
THERE WILL BE HOPES UNSPOKEN
AND JOYS TO HAUNT US STILL;
THERE WILL BE DAWN AND SUNSET
THOUGH WE HAVE CAST THE WORLD AWAY,
AND THE LEAVES DANCING
OVER THE HILL.

— JOHN GOULD FLETCHER (1886-1950)

introduction *town and gown*

IN MEMORY OF
EDGAR PALMER
WHOSE VISION AND GENEROSITY
PLANNED AND BUILT THIS SQUARE
FOR PRINCETON
WHICH HE SO LOVED

ERECTED BY HIS FRIENDS

When my husband, Doug, and I first moved to the Princeton area in 1978, we were captivated by its eastern sophistication, small-town charm, and historic elegance. A two-lane main road called Nassau Street split the town in half; locals liked to call it the "town and gown effect." Princeton University and several thousand students sat distinctively on the eastern side, while small family-owned shops opened their doors to "townies" on the west. Large shiny

the nassau inn

THE NASSAU INN (PRECEDING PAGE, RIGHT) WAS BUILT IN 1756, ORIGINALLY AS A DORM FOR COLLEGE STUDENTS. FAMOUS GUESTS HAVE INCLUDED PAUL REVERE, MEMBERS OF THE FIRST CONTINENTAL CONGRESS, AND SEVERAL SIGNERS OF THE DECLARATION OF INDEPENDENCE. ALBERT EINSTEIN JOINED NUMEROUS PRINCETON UNIVERSITY STUDENTS IN CARVING HIS NAME ON ONE OF THE OAK TABLES IN THE DOWNSTAIRS TAP ROOM.

DESIGNED BY RALEIGH C. GILDERSLEEVE TO MODEL SIXTEENTH-CENTURY HOUSES IN CHESTER, ENGLAND, THE ARCHITECTURALLY DISTINCTIVE UPPER AND LOWER PYNE BUILDINGS WERE BUILT AS GIFTS FROM MOSES TAYLOR PYNE IN 1896, WITH SHOPS ON THE FIRST FLOOR AND DORMITORY ROOMS FOR PRINCETON UNDERGRADUATES ON THE SECOND FLOOR. THE SURVIVING LOWER PYNE BUILDING (RIGHT), ON THE CORNER OF NASSAU AND WITHERSPOON, NOW HOUSES HAMILTON JEWELERS.

cars were parked at an angle, with parking meters few and far between. There were numerous small businesses, such as Clayton's Yarn Shop, Nassau Interiors, Davidson's Supermarket, Urken's Hardware, and the ever reliable Woolworth's. When we arrived on the East Coast, after my husband took a job in Manhattan, we had no idea where to live; the experience was like entering a foreign country. The locals talked fast, with heavy accents, and it was impossible to find good Mexican food anywhere. In desperation, we found an apartment in New Jersey and resorted to shipping our favorite Pace-brand hot sauce directly from the San Antonio factory—not an easy task in the days before UPS and Federal Express.

(LEFT) Like much of the country, Princetonians are consumed by good coffee—morning, noon, and night. Our numerous coffeehouses have become a gathering place for both students and residents, a place where town and gown meet.

(RIGHT) Princeton offers breakfast, lunch, and dinner at a variety of colorful ethnic restaurants.

(FOLLOWING PAGE LEFT AND RIGHT) A spring day on Witherspoon Street, with Nassau Hall peeking through the tops of flowering pear trees.

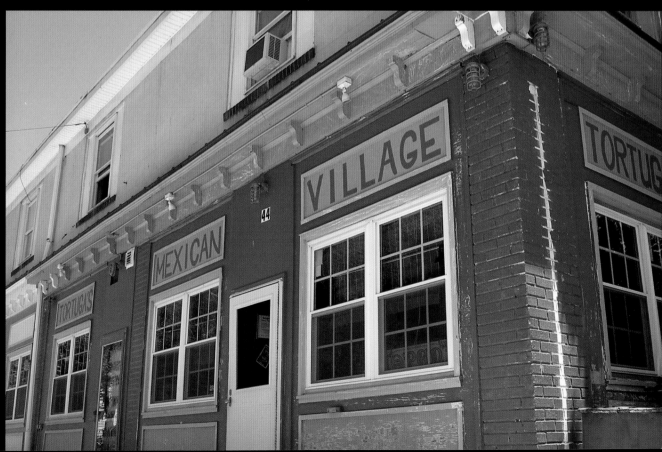

A few years later, we built our first home on Douglas Drive in the village of Kingston. We often drove the few miles down the King's Highway to explore Princeton's architecturally beautiful but rather quiet college town. There were no traditional Friday-night high school football games with marching band halftime shows. The only sign of life from the academic side of town was the annual parade of enthusiastic alumni wearing multi-patterned orange and black jackets, hats, and pants. We were Texas Longhorn fans, so orange was our favorite color, and we had hopes of fitting right in.

During shopping visits, as we tried to figure out what this Yankee culture was all about, I would treat myself to inexpensive bundles of freshly cut flowers from tiny Cox's

Market on Nassau Street. If the budget permitted, we would contemplate purchasing a wonderful cut of meat from Toto's Butcher Shop on Witherspoon Street. We were intrigued by the local residents, by their style of dress and the landscape of this small oasis in the center of New Jersey. We quickly realized that Princeton wasn't like the small towns we had known in Texas.

At the end of Nassau Street, the Olde English Shop marked the southernmost corner of town. In Texas, this was where you would have headed onto a rural farm road; exiting Princeton, you continued down a historical route past the Governor's Mansion and pre–Revolutionary War homes. In this preppy men's store, you could easily find a suitable bow tie and colorful plaid pants, should a member of your family be inclined to wear them.

Edith's Lingerie sat next to the Nassau Christian Church on the corner of Chambers Street and Nassau. I always found that amusing, since it never would have been allowed in any churchgoing neighborhood I knew of in Texas. Edith, however, was quite a lady and businesswoman. She was careful to never make her window displays too provocative, which might offend Sunday churchgoers. Her shop, like many others in town, was closed on Sunday. A trip to Edith's always guaranteed that a grandmotherly saleslady would efficiently fit you into the perfect undergarment for any occasion—it was better than the foundations department at Neiman Marcus in Dallas.

Just across from the main entrance to Princeton University, a large bronze tiger designed by sculptor Charles R. Knight welcomed visitors to Palmer Square, built by Edgar Palmer in 1937. The Nassau Inn, with its famous thirteen-foot *Yankee Doodle Dandy* mural painted by Norman Rockwell in 1937, anchored the Town Square. Inn guests can still have a drink in the Tap Room, but the delicious Sunday brunch in the

(LEFT) Each graduating class at Princeton University wears costumes until their fifteenth or twentieth reunion; class blazers and sometimes an umbrella with the class year until their fiftieth; and blazers or a simple hatband with the class year thereafter. David Loevner, Class of 1976, shared his distinguished attire during the year's Reunions Weekend celebrations.

(RIGHT TOP AND BOTTOM) The Mediterra Herban Garden, started four years ago as an organic restaurant garden. Designed and maintained by Peter Soderman, the small plot on Paul Robeson Place is a visual gift to the community from brothers Carlo and Raoul Momo, creators of the Witherspoon Bread Company, Theresa's Café, and Mediterra.

now-defunct Garden Room is a sweet memory; a Swiss chocolate shop has taken its place. The Princeton Playhouse, an enormous in-town movie theater (now sadly gone) filled the back corner of the square. The theater showed only one movie, as hard as that is to imagine. To my surprise, Princeton even offered a bowling alley for university students. It later became a disco club and now houses the Triumph Brewing Company.

As newcomers, Doug and I would often drive through the western section of town to view the elegant turn-of-the-century homes. The streets had prominent names, such as Cleveland Lane, Boudinot Street, Library Place, Hodge Road, and my favorite, the Great Road. I was certain that wealthy old Princetonians, all graduates of prestigious Ivy League schools and with pedigrees dating back to the *Mayflower*, occupied each of these grand houses.

So this was how Yankees lived, I thought: in small towns full of stately old mansions, with gentlemen walking to lunch at the private Nassau Club, wearing their bow ties with plaid pants and brightly colored blazers. White-haired ladies, perfectly groomed in Pendleton wool jackets, stockings, pumps, and square handbags, attended garden club meetings or proper bridge luncheons at the Present Day Club. No cowboy boots, Mexican restaurants, or Dairy Queens to be found.

While we still consider ourselves Texans, as we settled into our new home on Brearly Road, with our first child, we came to call

(LEFT) "We need bread and you gave us cake."—President Woodrow Wilson's response to Andrew Carnegie's refusal to endow either Princeton University's graduate school or the preceptorial system; instead, Carnegie donated funds to build a lake for the undergraduate rowing team. Created in 1906, Lake Carnegie is now an official Olympic training site for the 2004 and 2008 Summer Games. It is often used for community canoeing, sailing, and fishing, as well as skating in the winter.

(RIGHT) Our small link to the rest of the world: the Princeton Dinky train station. Dating as far back as 1865, this single-car train has been used by students and commuters and is known simply as the Dinky. The train station was once located on campus, and the archway of Princeton's Blair Hall and its grand staircase were the university's impressive main entrance. Students complained about the soot entering their dorms, so the new station was built in 1920.

Princeton home. Both of our sons were born at the local hospital, and they consider themselves Princetonians first and adopted Texans second. I feel fortunate to have found a second home that offers such a diverse experience in culture and American history, deep in the heart of the Garden State.

While Princeton has grown considerably over the past twenty years—the main stretch of Nassau Street is now four lanes, with metered parallel parking—it has managed to retain an atmosphere of neighborly warmth and belonging. This is a town where you know your neighbors, their children, and their pets. Kids walk or bike to town after school to get ice cream, pizza, or a hoagie. They feel safe, welcome, and comfortable as they walk down Nassau Street, often chatting with the local shopkeepers or restaurant owners.

(PRECEDING PAGE LEFT) Filled with works by notable Princeton authors old and new, Micawber Books, an independent bookstore, has been part of the heart of downtown Princeton for over twenty years. Its contemporary environment reflects the philosophy of owners Margaret Griffin and Logan Fox to read the best in literature.

(PRECEDING PAGE RIGHT) Worth the wait: It doesn't get better than buttermilk pancakes topped with strawberries and whipped cream served on the initial-inscribed tabletops at Pj's Pancake House. Weekend breakfast lines stretch out the door and down the street for this small café, which has become a breakfast tradition for visiting alumni, university students, and townies alike.

(LEFT) Princetonians love ice cream—just ask anyone waiting in the lines at Thomas Sweet or Halo Pub.

(LEFT) Along with a dedicated staff, Jack and Debbie Morrison, owners of the Nassau Street Seafood & Produce Company, often cook for thousands during Princeton University's Reunions Weekend. They offer the same gracious service and commitment to quality year-round. Long lines form each evening for coveted tables at their adjacent restaurant, the Blue Point Grill, managed by Steve Murray. Executive chef Brian Dougherty teaches us by example to prepare seafood in simple but delicious ways, following Jack's philosophy of "Fresh Fish—No Frou Frou."

(RIGHT) Students flock to local family-owned hangouts—Hoagie Haven, Pizza Star, Tiger Noodles, Conti's, George's Ribs and Roasters—all within walking distance of the university, Princeton High School, and the John Witherspoon Middle School.

On a glorious spring day two years ago, as I sat outside the Witherspoon Bread Company, once Toto's Butcher Shop, sipping coffee and enjoying croissants with my sweet-spirited cousin D. from Austin, she told me that coming to Princeton for the first time was like visiting Pleasantville—the ever so perfect town from the 1998 movie. The setting, she said, reminded her of gentle places like Springfield in *Father Knows Best* or Mayfield in *Leave It to Beaver*. I understood exactly what she meant.

Like most small towns in the United States, Princeton is in a constant state of transformation, blending the old with the new and welcoming people from all over the world to its academic and culturally diverse environment. As family-owned businesses succumb to retirements, changes in taste, or financial woes, entrepreneurial ideas have emerged that keep shopping, eating, and socializing in a constant cycle of birth. Now as you travel visually through town on Nassau Street, architect Michael Graves'

(LEFT) Princeton is diverse in
its religious beliefs and ethnic
backgrounds. The stained-glass
window of St. Paul's—one of the
community's many churches,
synogogues, and centers of
religious thought—is an
architectural treasure enjoyed
on a spring afternoon.

(RIGHT) Jardinière Florals fills its
Nassau Street sidewalk entrance
with seasonal displays, enticing
shoppers to explore.

professional offices and store welcome you at the Harrison Street intersection. On the weekend you can stop at the Blue Point Grill for dinner with pretty much everyone in town, or rent a movie and order Chinese, Greek, Thai, Japanese, or Indian takeout on mini–restaurant row, between Linden Lane and Chestnut Street. Whole Earth Center can sell you organic foods, or you can head back to Harrison Street and McCaffrey's Supermarket in the Princeton Shopping Center for a full week's groceries. While you're there, the Winged Pig will help you with a hostess or birthday gift, and Bon Appetit will round out the gourmet section of your pantry. After all that, if you're too tired to cook, the Main Street Bistro will offer you a chair in their outdoor café;

f you're in a hurry, you can grab a slice of pizza at Pizza Star, along with half the Little League baseball teams in town.

After you pick up your kids from sports practice a few blocks away at the John Witherspoon Middle School or the Princeton High School, then drop them off at the new public library for homework, you can select a book at Micawber Books. Then sit back and relax in one of the numerous coffee shops that line

Witherspoon and Nassau streets. Chances are, when your cell phone rings to pick the kids up a second time, they will now be hungry. Head back to Nassau Street for a cheesesteak from Hoagie Haven. Save dining at Pj's Pancake House for Sunday. Give in to a sit-down dinner only if the kids request sushi. Then take them to see Mr. Choi at Nassau Bagel Sushi, where they will notice the line at Thomas Sweet and, lucky for you, probably ask for ice cream with blend-ins.

After yielding numerous times to students and professors in the crosswalks, you exit Nassau Street and head toward the Governor's Mansion. Hopefully, there will be no public events tonight, and with little traffic, you will finally arrive home. The dog will want to go for a long evening walk along the canal, which sounds good until your husband calls for a ride home from the Dinky train station off Nassau Street. While you suggest he might enjoy the short walk home, you get back into the car and do the loop again. At the end of the day, you may find yourself heading for the Herban Garden, for a little quiet meditation.

(LEFT) Autumn's intense palette of leaf color.

(RIGHT) The McKinnons' snow-covered Chinese-red gazebo on Edgerstoune Road.

(FOLLOWING PAGE) Princeton Battlefield State Park, spring 2002.

For years, we have taken our children to Texas in the summer so they can experience our home state, its food, gracious citizens, and casual entertaining style. When we return from these vacations and turn off Stockton Street to wind down narrow Edgerstoune Road, I roll down my window to welcome the cool evening breeze and hear the welcome-back chorus of the cicadas. We pass Michelle Seass' "Little House on the Road" and Marty McKinnon's soothing Chinese-red gazebo floating on a small pond. As we pass through the Russell Estates stone and iron entrance gates onto Winant Road and begin our turn onto Brearly Road, we always check on the progress of the restoration of the old Russell mansion. After the searing days of a Texas August, where temperatures stay above the hundred-degree mark, the Princeton night air has a comforting crispness, which reminds me that the colorful leaves of autumn and the deep snows of winter are on their way. I know that we have returned to another wonderful place we call home, to a house where my sons were once babies, where the rooms are full of memories with friends and family.

"You know how some houses seem happy when you walk in them, and some carry such an overtone of melancholy, they seem cold even on a hot day? I believe everyone who lives in a place leaves an imprint on the place itself. Your house is, after all, you."

—Gladys Tabor, *Stillmeadow and Sugarbridge,*1953

Debbie Tunnell
September 2004

fay's sacred space *a mother's legacy*

Every child is an artist. The problem is how to remain an artist once he grows up.

— PABLO PICASSO (1881–1973)

diligently over her students in a painting within a painting. The original now resides in a private collection with several other Sciarra creations, including a very special piece called *Sacred Space*.

Fay makes contemporary art that is personal, heartfelt, and spiritual, with intricate patterns, imaginative details, and bold colors. Much of her subject matter is autobiographical, about the small moments in life that ultimately give it meaning. Fay calls her style "embellished reality"; she also calls it "sophisticated naïve." Many of her works are painted on found objects, such as vintage washboards and windows. She scavenges local flea markets and antique shops for unique items to transfigure into art.

The story of how Fay became an artist is a blend of family memories and a celebration of the creativity that lies within us all. While her mother, Suzanne, battled cancer, she offered to her youngest daughter a legacy that would be fulfilled through art. Suzanne had always painted, though just for pleasure. As

(LEFT) The 1921 stucco Tudor was built from plans out of a Sears catalog.

her life came to an end, she passed on her treasured brushes to Fay, telling her quite simply that she should paint. A television producer living in California, Fay had never dreamed of becoming an artist. But at thirty-eight, on her son's first birthday—almost a year to the day since her mother had passed away—she picked up the collection of paintbrushes, bought a few tubes of paint, and began a journey that would change her life.

In the spring of 2001, Dale and I visited Fay's studio to discuss a planned party that would christen her new space, and to take a peek at *Hookers*. Her stucco Tudor home, on a narrow side street in the village of Lawrence, was built in 1921 from plans out of the Sears catalog. Fay and her husband, David, created a new look using an unusual color—a soft Tuscan coral—Fay's self-designed verdigris attic grate covers, and cottage-style landscaping with bountiful window boxes. You might, however, happen upon the basic house plan in numerous other neighborhoods throughout the United States.

The house and adjacent studio over the garage tell you instantly that you've entered an artist's domain. A collaboration between Fay and architect Ron Berlin, the studio was completed in the summer of 2000. Fay's vision was to echo the lines of the main house and create an unusual, inspiring cross between an attic

(ABOVE) The invitation, designed by Dale and by Lynne Wildenboer, features a transparency of Fay's painting *Sacred Space*.
The font captured her signature style, and the colors were taken from the original oil painting.

and a church. Numerous architectural elements were incorporated, including stained glass, columns, a garden fence, and a functional old claw-foot bathtub.

Fay's home and studio walls are filled with numerous thought-provoking paintings that reflect her passage from daughter mourning the loss of her mother to accomplished artist with a message about life, family, and spirituality. The studio is both captivating and inspiring; I almost thought I could start painting in such an environment. And if I needed to meditate and ponder what my subject would be, a bubbly soak in the antique bathtub with a glass of champagne would probably help me on my way. Filled with birch tree beams, vintage doors, and a creaky old iron daybed stacked with soft linen coverlets, this is truly Fay's sacred space. But it was the painting of her studio on an old church window, capturing the feeling of this space, that caught my eye. I knew, and Dale agreed, that the painting had to be part of our invitation for the celebration. It became the title of our book.

(LEFT) Fay's artistic touch begins at her front door. Along with the vibrant Tuscan colors, a vintage chair filled with spring flowers and a tiered birdhouse designed and painted by Sam Miller, welcome guests.

(RIGHT) Completed in the summer of 2000, the second-floor garage studio, designed by local architect Ron Berlin, was a collaboration with Fay. Her vision was to echo the lines of the main house and create a cross between an attic and a church.

And that's where our journey began. Originally scheduled for late September 2001, the party was held on Mother's Day weekend of 2002, which seemed appropriate. Fay's May garden was lush with blooms—late-blooming spring bulbs and early-summer roses— and the weather cooperated. Over one hundred friends, family, and media attended the afternoon garden cocktail party. As the young cellist played and the sushi chef created, and our favorite chef, Ed Batejan, filled platters in the kitchen with a selection of delicious hors d'oeuvres, we celebrated the completion of a space that represents professional and personal success and happiness, and a daughter fulfilling her mother's gift and dream.

(LEFT TOP) John Giammearse and Eric Roberts of Jardinière Florals on Nassau Street filled inexpensive glass compotes with perfect-colored roses and galax leaves. This simple but sophisticated combination accented rather than competing with the May garden.

(LEFT CENTER) Lauren Engelbert, right, and her friends, Nina DeReuter and Caitlin Rhoades greeted guests.

(LEFT BOTTOM) Spicy Wavy Tortilla Chips.

(RIGHT) Fay Sciarra greets arriving guests with a colorful palette of hors d'oeuvres.

(LEFT) An early-morning visit to the Philadelphia produce market one week prior to the party yielded a selection of garnishes for each serving tray. Ed's special recipe for salmon was the beginning of an incredible quesadilla. Fresh flour tortillas—a local treat from the Central Market in Austin, Texas—were filled with marinated, smoked, and grilled salmon; fresh mozzarella; caramelized onions; and red peppers. The quesadillas were topped with a spicy fresh salsa made of pineapple, mango, jalapeños, and cilantro.

(RIGHT) We splurged on baby lamb chops with a fresh tomato-mint relish, but we also included the more economical, if unusual, fig-and-Gorgonzola-cheese-stuffed phyllo triangles.

take-out

WE MADE A DECISION TO SERVE ONLY CHAMPAGNE PUNCH
AND RED AND WHITE WINE, ALONG WITH SPARKLING LEMON
WATER AND SODA. WITH SUCH A SIZEABLE CROWD, A FULL
BAR WOULD HAVE BEEN EXPENSIVE AND DIDN'T SET THE
RIGHT TONE FOR A GARDEN GATHERING.

BECAUSE OF SPACE LIMITATIONS, MOST OF THE FOOD WAS
PREPPED IN ADVANCE AND COOKED AT FAY'S. BUT RATHER
THAN CLOSE OFF THE KITCHEN, WE DECIDED TO LET GUESTS
ENJOY WATCHING THE FOOD BE CREATED.

EACH PERSON ATTENDING THE OPENING OF THE STUDIO
RECEIVED A WINEGLASS HAND-PAINTED BY FAY.

party week

Entertaining large numbers of guests requires a great deal of organization and is a rewarding but exhausting experience, even for a professional. For Fay's party, I kept a diary of the highs and lows of our pre-party week. This brief behind-the-scenes look is a reminder that a well-planned party should bring a feeling of accomplishment to everyone involved.

(LEFT) Fay borrowed back many of her original works to create a once-in-a-lifetime show. Paintings were scattered throughout the garden on easels, and hung on the fence, house, and studio walls.

monday

Shopped for ingredients for appetizers and dessert. E-mailed Fay on Sunday night, checking on the progress of the new patio and landscaping. Promised her that Dale and I would stop by on Tuesday to view the results.

tuesday

Made peanut-brittle bars to freeze. Dale and I met with Fay and were delighted with the stone patio addition to her studio. It will make a perfect entrance and offer a place to gather during the party. Fay's home is full of art. She has asked galleries and friends to lend back her work in order to fill the garden, house, and studio walls with paintings. The garden chairs that we purchased at a local thrift store looked perfect with the table Fay found at the flea market. Discussed flow of party and style of dress for the evening. Promised to come back on Friday afternoon for another walk-through and to answer any last-minute questions.

(LEFT TOP) Crab and Capellini Balls with Jalapeño-Lime Sauce.

(LEFT CENTER) Sushi platter.

(LEFT BOTTOM) Fig-and-Gorgonzola-Cheese-Stuffed Phyllo Triangles.

sushi tale

SUSHI CHEF ANDY YEH WON A GOLD MEDAL AT THE 2002 WASHINGTON, D.C., CHERRY BLOSSOM FESTIVAL. AT OUR FIRST MEETING, I OPENED A RECENTLY PURCHASED SUSHI COOKBOOK WITH PICTURES OF WHAT I THOUGHT WERE EXQUISITE SQUARES OF MAKI WITH DYED RICE IN VIBRANT COLORS AND DESIGNS. ANDY CHUCKLED AND POLITELY HANDED US HIS PORTFOLIO. I REALIZED AFTER THE FIRST PHOTO THAT I SHOULD RETURN THE BOOK. WE HAD OUR EXPERT, AND HE WAS AN ARTIST WITH FRESH FISH, RICE, AND SEAWEED. AS EXPECTED, THE SUSHI AND SASHIMI TABLE WAS VERY POPULAR.

wednesday

Tired after making stuffing for phyllo triangles last night and cutting peanut-brittle bars. Have to work on recipe to make that easier. Maybe I'll cut them while warm next time. Will fill phyllo triangles and freeze to bake on Saturday. Asked my cousin to bring back fresh flour tortillas from the Central Market in Austin. Not sure if they'll make it onto the plane. If not, will use local tortillas. Still working on a musician. Budget is tight—hoping for a high school student to play the harp, cello, or guitar.

thursday

Still looking for a musician. Not giving up, though. Friend assures me someone will volunteer, but it is AP test week at the high school. Labeling all food trays to make it easier for servers. Cooked the Spicy Wavy Tortilla Strips and sealed in large plastic container so they would stay crisp.

(LEFT) Our friend Jane Moni designed and painted the colorful pansy platter, which beautifully displayed zucchini fritters topped with crème fraîche and caviar and garnished with soft chive blossoms.

friday

Weather prediction is still very good, but it's New Jersey: can't trust the weather until the morning of the party! Dale and I head over to Fay's at four p.m. to calm her pre-party jitters. While there, we set up the round tables and help Fay decide where to display the outside art tomorrow morning. Her home, studio, and garden look absolutely beautiful. Fay and David have splurged on cleaning ladies, who arrive while we're there, and whiz through the rooms. We sit outside enjoying a perfect spring evening and drink a toast to success.

(RIGHT) *Hookers* by Fay Sciarra.

saturday

Dale and I are weary but look forward to our first book party. Fay's kitchen is buzzing with activity, and the prep of platters for the photographer goes well. The unique collection of garnishes we selected at the produce market is still available on Friday, so the planned pre-party photo shoot of the food moves quickly. With guests scheduled to arrive in fifteen minutes, Dale and I hurry to change and join the party. After almost a year's planning of this event, over a hundred have said yes, the weather prediction is 70 degrees and sunny, and Fay is very excited about sharing this once-in-a-lifetime collection of her work with friends and family.

(LEFT) Just outside the entrance to Fay's studio, cellist Sara Wolfe set the tone for the party with a selection of classical music.

(RIGHT) Fay's sacred space.

birds of a feather *and Ruby Pearl*

What art offers is space, a certain
breathing room for the spirit.

— JOHN UPDIKE (1932–)

Special
Clothing
Show
5-8 p.m.

*W*hat a combination this party turned out to be: three artistic New Jersey shopkeepers and a young clothing designer from Texas. As with many of our favorite parties, this one was the result of a last-minute inspiration from Shelley Roe, Ann Battle, and Marci Kahn, former owners of Birds of a Feather in Kingston, New Jersey. After meeting my cousin's daughter Sunny, an Austin-based clothing designer, at Fay Sciarra's party in May, they had invited her back to Princeton for a late-spring trunk show. Sunny is a talented and artistic young woman with an eclectic style; her studies have taken her to the School of the Art Institute of Chicago, the New York School of Visual Arts, and back home to the University of Texas at Austin. While her background

WOLF
MODEL
FORM
CO.

74S
PATENTS PENDING

ODEL 1945

12

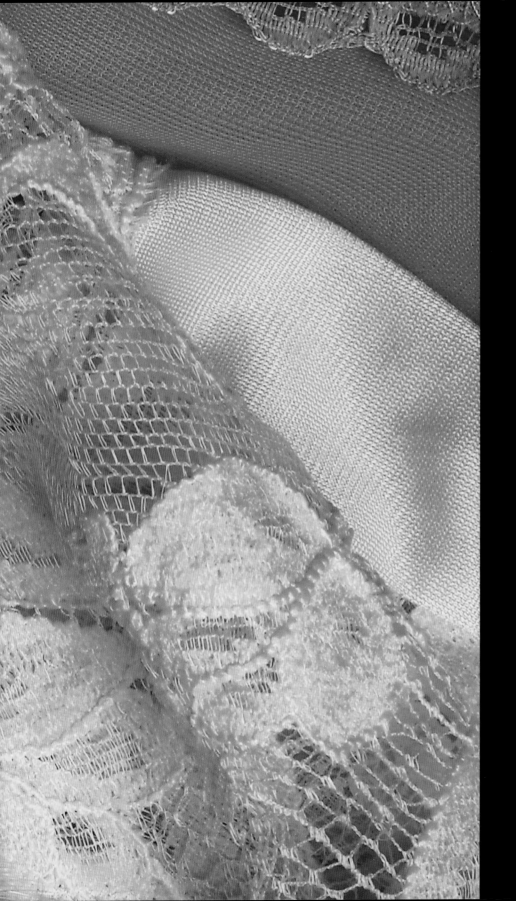

in mixed media and illustration compelled her to create thought-provoking paintings and sculpture, it also led her to design dresses out of vintage slips. Before she knew it, her creations were selling out in the funky Austin boutiques, and she was home in her post-war three-room cottage, sewing

(PRECEDING PAGE) Designers Sunny Haralson and Chia Guillory

(ABOVE) Easter bonnet attitude—Sunny with Granny Pearl.

(LEFT) Ruby Pearl vintage slip designs are playful, colorful, and bold.

a collection of dresses for an upcoming fashion show. Word about her camisoles and dresses got around quickly in the Austin music scene. She soon found herself stitching old slips into one-of-a-kind creations for singer Patti Griffin and other Texas musicians.

Sunny calls her line of clothing Ruby Pearl, a tribute to her maternal grandmother, whom I knew as Aunt Pearl. To my surprise, Ruby Pearl Seaton was apparently quite a seamstress. I remember her only as a dear, sweet, smoking, cussing, large Texas woman who drank beer and could fill a room with her raucous laughter. She was usually laughing about something naughty, and my mother often tried to shoo my cousin Diane and me out of the room when things got a little too entertaining for our tender young ears.

(LEFT) Aunt Pearl's spirit was as well known as her biscuits and gravy and handmade aprons.

(RIGHT) Patti Griffin wears Ruby Pearl designs on the jacket of her 2003 release, *1000 Kisses.*

I was my parents' fourth child and only daughter, and Diane was the sweet younger sister I had always wanted. We were—and still are after many years apart—close and connected, even though our lives have taken very different paths. It amazes me that this soft-spoken, pensive woman, who now teaches yoga as a hobby, was born to two such boisterous, outgoing individuals as Aunt Pearl and my mother's brother, Uncle Andy. I guess sometimes the apple does fall far from the tree. Or maybe the huge outstretched limbs just overshadow it, and it rolls away, ready to find a place to take root and grow.

Rumor had it that Aunt Pearl carried a pistol in her purse until the day she died, in case there was trouble brewing. In her younger years, she rode a Harley-Davidson and knew a wide array of colorful characters in her earlier years. It was rumored that she owned a bar called the Magic Lounge on the infamous Jacksboro Highway, and that her mother, Ruby, had entertained Bonnie and Clyde in her modest house on Crump Street in the historic stockyards section of Fort Worth, Texas. Born in that house in 1927, Pearl had her childhood cut short by the Depression. She left school in the third grade to cook all the family meals, while

her mother, father, and three brothers worked the cotton fields. Pearl's biscuits and gravy were legendary, as was her desire to learn to read. Self-taught, Aunt Pearl read every book and magazine she could get her hands on. She also loved to write letters. Despite her inability to spell correctly, she composed weekly letters to her daughter and kept a diary of her inner thoughts and experiences.

I'm almost certain I learned the word "honky-tonk" from Aunt Pearl. She used the word often. As a child, I believed that the Texas-brewed Pearl beer must have been named after her or was at least in her honor. I was

(LEFT) Birds of a Feather in Kingston.

(RIGHT) Susan designed whimsical, in-store signage that was displayed on vintage hangers to promote the upcoming trunk show.

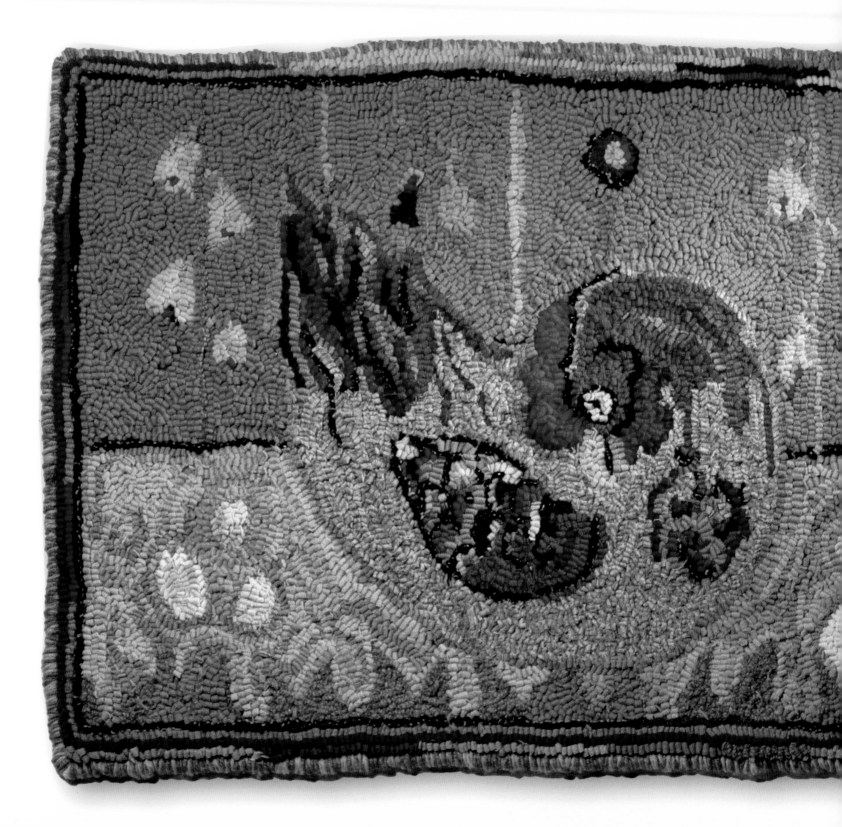

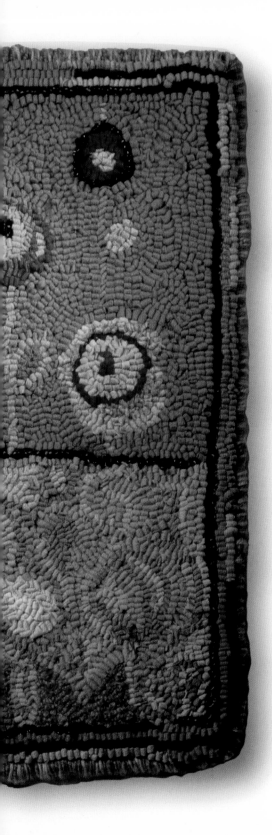

sure that was why she always had a bottle nearby. Thanks to her, I learned to giggle at jokes that made my mother blush and my grandma Wheeler laugh until she could hardly breathe. I also came to understand that while a religious woman such as my mother could never approve of Pearl's seemingly decadent lifestyle, she had a love for this wild Texas lady that would never cease, even after Pearl and Andy divorced.

Until I reconnected in Austin with Diane and her daughter Heather Sunrise in 1998, I never knew my aunt had loved to sew. Aunt Pearl passed on her talent for designing beautiful clothes to her youngest granddaughter. Born in 1975, Sunny loved sewing and learning to cuss with Granny Pearl. They spent their time together cutting out patterns and stitching away, using an old electric Singer that Diane had purchased at a pawnshop as Pearl's Mother's Day present when Sunny was only two years old. Sadly, Pearl passed away in 1995 at age sixty-nine.

In June 2002 I watched Sunny anxiously unpacking her numerous suitcases in my Princeton guest room. As she laid out all the colorful clothes she had brought for the trunk show, I imagined Aunt Pearl smiling down on all of us, checking out the wild designs her grandchild had created. I am sure that had she been there with us, she would have tried to stuff her womanly body into one of them, if only for a laugh or two.

Imagination is the

true magic carpet.

(LEFT) A hooked rug by Shelley Roe.

— NORMAN VINCENT PEALE (1898-1993)

quaint village

As I think back on this party, I realize that Birds of a Feather was the perfect setting for Sunny to showcase her artistic talents. Opened in 1996 and, sadly, closed in 2004, Birds was the brainchild of a trio of friends who decided to locate their singular store in Kingston. In this quaint village, adjacent to the Delaware and Raritan Canal, several shopkeepers have created a nest of stores that draw shoppers out of Princeton and up the road a few miles. A distinctive style and architecture, along with a hand-carved sign, let you know that you've exited Princeton and entered the historic village of Kingston, established in 1675. A plaque at the top of the hill by the cemetery commemorates George Washington's journey along the King's Highway (now known as Route 27)

(LEFT) Colorful tags designed by Susan, strung on a vintage hanger, identified the tempting hors d'oeuvres placed throughout the store.

(RIGHT) Becky Rauch models a garment designed by Ruby Pearl.

through Kingston during the Battle of Princeton in 1777. The village was a major stagecoach stop during the 1800s, and the inn that housed weary travelers still stands on a corner, awaiting restoration.

Across from Birds of a Feather is Main Street Bakery and Coffeehouse, a bistro-style café that opened in 1984 in what was the old village grocery store. Owner Sue Simpkins's cozy space is a mainstay for delicious homemade sandwiches, salads, soups, and desserts and is a great gathering spot. A true barbershop with a revolving red and white pole, a tiny and never crowded post office, a small but welcoming Methodist church, the Kingston flower shop, and a bridle and saddle shop complete this one-block village. There are no supermarkets, fast-food chains, or gas stations in sight.

At the bottom of the hill, just before Princeton, stands the lock tender's house for the Delaware and Raritan Canal. Completed in 1834, the D&R Canal's towpath has been converted to a lovely seventy-mile trail for joggers, walkers, and bikers. The view of adjacent Carnegie Lake is

(LEFT) While designed for the young at heart, Sunny's designs were destined to be worn by teenage models such as Lauren Engelbert and Becky Rauch.

(RIGHT) Wearing a Ruby Pearl camisole, Anne Battle, one of the owners of Birds of a Feather, admires a reversible hat by designer Chia Guillory.

peaceful and serene, no matter what time of year. But my favorite season is autumn, when the trees' striking colors reflect in the water and the path is covered with red, orange, and yellow leaves. A small dam at the end of Lake Carnegie creates a mini waterfall, and the tranquil sound of the rushing water is mesmerizing.

The Kingston gristmill sits perched at the edge of Route 27. Built in the mid-1800s and part of the nationally registered historic district, the mill has a spectacular view of the waterfall, towpath, and Lake Carnegie. Just west of Kingston is a small restored gentleman's farmhouse called Rockingham, where George Washington wrote his farewell to his troops in 1783. After advancing to Kingston following the Battle of Princeton, Washington ordered his troops to burn the town's bridge, halting Lord Cornwallis and the British army. Except for the occasional dump truck carrying stone from the quarry nearby, Kingston is today a peaceful little village, and shoppers travel there often to enjoy the atmosphere. On the corner of the King's Highway and Ridge Road sits one of the town's landmarks: the distinctive pink-lavender-and-green-painted Victorian home that housed Birds of a Feather.

Birds of a Feather offered vintage home furnishings, jewelry, and the latest finds from flea markets all over the world. Shelley and Ann are artists, collectors, and creators of unique hand-painted pieces for the home. Shelley designs and creates one-of-a-kind hand-hooked wool rugs, while Ann and Marci have a knack for finding the latest hot artist from Paris, Maine, or Martha's Vineyard. The store was a plethora of creativity and fun, and you couldn't walk away without a treasure or two.

ladie's night

I was thrilled for the opportunity to sponsor Sunny's impromptu trunk show at my friends' store. I thought this yin and yang of talent would be the source of a wonderful ladies' night out with good food, drinks, shopping, and conversation. Mothers and daughters came together. The moms shopped Birds' unique gifts, while the girls tried on the vintage hand-dyed slip dresses, custom jewelry, hats, and purses. Sunny

(LEFT) Main Street Bakery and Coffeehouse.

(RIGHT) Lou's Barbershop.

(FOLLOWING PAGE LEFT) Locks on the Delaware and Raritan Canal.

(FOLLOWING PAGE RIGHT) A lone fisherman near the Kingston gristmill and the Carnegie Lake dam.

(LEFT) Sliced beef tenderloin rounds were topped with homemade horseradish sauce and surrounded by the pink and blue designs of Baby Buda.

(ABOVE) Roasted garlic aioli and miniature crab cakes.

brought along her friend Chia Guillory, a successful Austin-based designer of sundresses and reversible handbags and hats. Chia brought along her mother's baby-clothing designs, called Baby Buda, after a tiny Texas town. Once word had spread through Austin's design scene that there would be an East Coast trunk show, numerous designers sent goodies: jewelry, more handbags, sachets, and aprons—the list grew quite long. The shop was bursting with merchandise. In fact, the trunk show brought in

so much talent from the Texas state capital that it continued for two additional days. Friends of Birds showed up to share in the excitement generated by this cross-country event. Upstairs and down were both packed with people.

I enjoyed preparing this menu on short notice and had fun placing it throughout the store's cupboards, dressing tables, and antique furniture. Nonalcoholic piña coladas were served on the front porch for the teenagers, along with white wine for the adults. As shoppers searched for treasures amid the store's new merchandise, they were rewarded with a taste of something out of the ordinary, just like the evening.

I wanted to create a menu with a few special touches that reflected the vintage location and the colorful style of these talented women. A baked Brie was filled with caramelized onions and peppers, wrapped in puff pastry, and topped with a paper-doll-like cutout dress, mimicking a Ruby Pearl design. Cherry

(PRECEDING PAGE LEFT) Short on time, we kept the desserts simple. The 1940s Rootin'-Tootin'-Cowgirl-Shootin' fabric added a little cheesecake.

(PRECEDING PAGE RIGHT) Mother's antique ivy pot from England was filled with jicama sticks and garnished with fresh cilantro.

(LEFT) *Sally's Paranoia*, a painting on canvas by artist Fay Sciarra, stands guard over a "Dressed" Baked Brie.

(RIGHT) It was too crowded in the small Victorian house to pass hors d'oeuvres, so we tucked them into the store's antique cupboards and set them on top of vintage tables and chairs.

simply stradivarius *a tale of a few fiddles*

*After silence, that which comes nearest
to expressing the inexpressible is music.*

— ALDOUS HUXLEY (1894–1963)

If food is the way to one's heart, then music must hold a key to the soul. This is the tale of a few "fiddles," as their collector affectionately called them, and their journey from the workshops of sixteenth- and seventeenth-century Italian master fiddle makers Antonio and Girolamo Amati, Antonio Stradivari, and Giuseppe Guarneri del Gesu to their twenty-first-century destination in the hands of grateful New Jersey Symphony Orchestra musicians. But it is also the story of

(ABOVE) Cynthia and Rob Hillas.

the space within each of us that allows the enchanting and sometimes haunting sounds of the stringed instrument to release feelings so intense that they can be either pleasing or painful to experience. This musical therapy can calm or stir the soul, allowing its listener to silently sense what is often buried deep inside.

Sometimes in the simplest of ways, we are unexpectedly offered the opportunity to be part of a much bigger picture. In May 2002, my friend Cynthia Hillas asked me to help her plan an evening of music performed in her home by the New Jersey Symphony Orchestra. Little did either of us know the magnitude of what we were getting ourselves into. I had no idea of the importance of this gathering of more than a hundred local patrons of the arts; nor did I realize that we would all be in the company of four irreplaceable musical instruments. But after reading a *Wall Street Journal* article describing a New Jersey philanthropist's offer to sell the symphony his prized collection of twenty-four Italian violins, two violas, and four cellos created in the seventeenth and eighteenth centuries, I understood that this would be an uncommon gathering. With no time to waste, we began planning a memorable evening that would be called "Simply Stradivarius."

(PRECEDING PAGE) A striking red treble clef tops our trademark black-caviar torte.

(LEFT) Bacon-Wrapped Grissini: These caramelized bacon-wrapped breadsticks disappear quickly and are one of our most popular hors d'oeuvres.

(RIGHT TOP) A comfortable elegance. Food, linens, and flowers were selected to complement the extraordinary evening of music. Annie B's treble-clef chocolate shortbread cookies were stunning on a silver tray.

(RIGHT CENTER) Annie B's assorted mini-tarts: Tasty bites of summer.

(RIGHT BOTTOM) Pat's Spinach Buttons. Chef Ed Batejan borrowed his mother's recipe for spinach stuffing to create a delectable new hors d'oeuvre. We named them in her honor.

(FOLLOWING PAGE LEFT) The evening's program, designed by Susan, also incorporated a swirling musical quality.

(FOLLOWING PAGE RIGHT) Shrimp with tangy cocktail sauce.

an evening of comfortable elegance

In keeping with the spirit of the event, I knew that Cynthia would want a luxurious gathering. Every detail, from the tablecloths for the thirty-six-inch-round cocktail tables to the type of chairs, had to reflect the grandeur of these instruments and the New Jersey Symphony Orchestra. The musical program was planned for the end of the evening, which meant that the new family room would be filled with chairs. An outdoor tent would be necessary, both for shade and in case of bad weather. I might have opted for a clear tent, to allow the tall trees and green plantings of the Hillas's backyard to be part of the overall atmosphere, but we were experiencing extreme outside temperatures that week, and we worried that a clear tent would be like encasing everyone in plastic wrap for a few hours. So, Brian Richardson of L&A Tents suggested we switch to an all-white tent, with portable commercial air conditioners blowing at each end. This would provide a shaded spot where guests could mingle until the indoor concert.

With warm weather in mind, we selected a floral tablecloth in soft greens and lavenders from Special Occasions and kept everything else a crisp white, for an illusion of coolness. Ballroom chairs in a natural wood with soft neutral cushions were perfect for the tented terrace and offered guests a place to sit and enjoy the food and garden atmosphere. Torches were added to keep summer's pesky

(LEFT) Members of the New Jersey Symphony Orchestra. Left to right: Eric Wyrick, concertmaster, 1716 Guarnerius del Gesu Serdet; Adriana Rosin, first violin, 1685 Stradivari; Frank Foerster, principal viola, 1620 Antonius & Hieronimus Amati; and Johnathan Spitz, principal cello, 1969 Stradivari ex–Prince Gursky.

(RIGHT) *Picasso, Not Picasso* by Joan Goldsmith of Livingston, New Jersey. Each year the New Jersey Symphony Orchestra commissions twelve visual artists through its Art Strings program to create individual works of art using musical instruments as their canvas. These combinations of the visual and aural senses are auctioned at symphony events.

(FOLLOWING PAGE) A group of four decorated instruments by Antonio Stradivari: three violins and one cello. Left to right, the instruments are: The "Hellier" violin, 1679; the "Ole Bull" violin, 1687; the "Greffuhle" violin, c. 1700; the "Marylebone" Cello, 1688.
PHOTO COURTESY OF SHINICHI YOKOYAMA.

the secrets of
the forest of violins

the golden age collection

Antonio Stradivari (1644–1737), the most well known of the Italian violin makers, worked in Cremona, Italy, until his death at the age of ninety-three. Along with Andrea Guarneri, he apprenticed with the master violin maker Nicola Amati. He established his own workshop in Cremona in 1684. With a remarkably innate understanding of geometry and design, this craftsman searched throughout Italy, Albania, and Yugoslavia for wooden beams from collapsed bridges and houses. Stradivari wanted to make his instruments out of wood that was already one to two hundred years old and had been tempered by the fires that heated homes. He created more than eleven hundred instruments during his lifetime, and many believe the aged wood to be the source of their distinctive tone. Musicians describe the tone of each note, as well as those of Amati's and Guarneri's instruments, as "ringing on forever." Stradivari made his last violin the year of his death. Sadly, the string quartet didn't become popular until after he died, so he never heard this combination of his instruments played together. This might explain why he created just a handful of cellos and violas.

There are numerous other theories as to why the instruments made by Stradivari, Amati, and Guarneri achieve such superior sounds compared to contemporary instruments. In addition to the skill and training of these craftsmen, one popular belief is that violin makers of the late seventeenth and eighteenth centuries used a secret ingredient in their varnish, which

preserved the wood from insect borers. My favorite theory is based on the Maunder Minimum, a period from 1645 to 1715 A.D. According to Henri D. Grissino-Mayer in the Laboratory of Tree-Ring Science at the University of Tennessee, "Dramatic changes in climate affected the growth rate of trees in the Forest of the Violins in the eastern part of Trentino, Italy. This region is known among violin makers for its fir trees of resonance. Stradivari and his fellow Italian violin makers used this forest in the southern tip of the Alps as their source for spruce wood," which is the preferred wood for the top of the violin.

During a period of long winters and cold summers, there were reduced sunspots, with less intense radiation and extremely cold weather throughout most of Western Europe. The slow growth rate during this mini–Ice Age produced trees that had narrow rings, which ultimately strengthened the wood, creating a material that could never be duplicated. In other words, this extraordinary group of gifted Italian violin makers, working with irreplaceable wood, created instruments that cannot be matched. This temporarily unique period of climatic change lasted only about ninety-five years. As fate would have it, Antonio Stradivari was born one year before the Maunder Minimum began.

(LEFT) Members of the New Jersey Symphony Orchestra with the Golden Age Collection. PHOTO COURTESY OF THIERRY DEFONTAINES.

pins and needles *finding comfort in the art of the needle*

We sleep, but the loom of life never sleeps
and the pattern which was weaving when the sun went down
is weaving when it comes up tomorrow.

— HENRY WARD BEECHER (1813–1887)

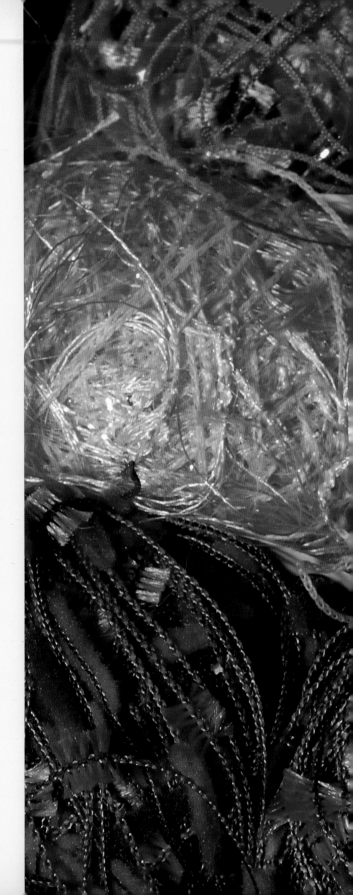

*S*ometimes life has a way of sneaking up from behind, giving us a good hard shake, and demanding that we take a look outside the comfortable and safe community that embraces each of us. It compels us to see and accept the extremes of the world, both good and bad. Such was the case for all of us in September 2001.

Menu

CAVIAR PIE
with Quilted Top

BOODLE WRAPPED SHRIMP
with Spicy Asian Dipping Sauce

POTATO ROLL-STORY PANCAKES
topped with Red Pepper Cream

SAFFRON-INFUSED SCALLOPS
with Golden Crème Fraiche

CHIPOTLE CHICKEN SATES
with Cilantro Dipping Sauce

CONFETTI CORN CAKES
with Roasted Tomato Relish

KATHLEEN'S SPICED PECANS

CHOCOLATE TRUFFLE QUILT CAKE

BUTTON SUGAR COOKIES

No one could have known that my friend Kathleen Gittleman's dream of opening a knitting, needlepoint, and quilting store in the heart of downtown Princeton would collide with such a catastrophic event as September 11. Nor could anyone have predicted that the timing of this pursuit would provide such a source of comfort for all of us in a moment of extreme confusion and intense pain. Yet in a space that once housed an art gallery, and now as part of a grouping of eclectic, small stores that have transformed tiny Chambers Street—such as Go for Baroque, Be in Style, Joy Cards, the Gilded Lion, and now Pins and Needles—Kathleen and her partner, Rachel Herr, successfully established a business that, on that day and for months to come, provided an invaluable outlet for the inherent need to keep our hands busy.

They say timing is everything, and that was certainly the case for the opening of this store. On Friday, September 7, 2001, Kathleen and Rachel opened the door at 8 Chambers Street for their first day. Only four months after making the decision to launch a new retail store, and after a summer of renovations and a flurry of trade shows and inventory orders, the two

(LEFT) Kathleen Gittleman and Rachel Herr, owners of Pins and Needles.

(FOLLOWING PAGE LEFT AND RIGHT) The turquoise-and-black Pins and Needles shopping bag inspired our invitation theme. Susan collaborated with her mother to embellish each. Using her art of the needle, Veronica Szymanski added unique, vintage buttons and zigzag stitching to the handmade invitations and menu.

entrepreneurs had opened for business. Still apprehensive about such a huge investment of time and money, they were immediately overwhelmed by the positive response of the Princeton area and the surrounding communities. Opening day found members of a local needlepoint guild perched on the narrow sidewalk, eager to enter their new source for exquisite yarns and canvases.

But within days, Kathleen and Rachel also welcomed stranded New York City residents and visitors from all over the world, seeking refuge from the tumult of September 11. Anxiously waiting for the trains to run again, for the tunnels and airports to reopen, customers searched through colorful bins of yarn and crowded walls of needlepoint canvases to keep themselves busy until they could return home. Trapped in our small town with no idea how or when they could return to their city, they also sought reassurance as they walked into the store and solemnly searched, sometimes for hours, for a knitting, needlepoint, or quilting project. Kathleen and Rachel not only offered their expertise and guidance, they also extended a comforting hand.

kismet on chambers street

Take your needle, my child,

and work at your pattern;

it will come out a rose by and by.

Life is like that—

one stitch at a time taken patiently

and the pattern will come out all right

like the embroidery.

— OLIVER WENDELL HOLMES (1809-1894)

What was once was a month of new beginnings instantly became connected to a time of overwhelming sadness for our nation and community. My oldest son celebrates his birthday in late September, and the weather has usually been glorious—early fall, with bright sunshine and crystal-clear deep blue skies, comfortably warm during the day and crisply cool at night. Princeton buzzes as families return from summer vacations, school days begin, and parents race to fill empty cupboards and backpacks with supplies. But now there is an unspoken grief haunting each of us as the anniversary of that day approaches. Flags appear and church bells ring. As a few years have passed, we have somehow found a place to store the fear and helplessness that consumed us all on that horrific morning. And for the most part, we have resumed new "normal" day-to-day lives, however deeply changed. But I suspect that for each generation, and especially for our children's, September 11 will forever be a part of our world in a very defining way. For our children, the day the Twin Towers fell, the day our nation's skies were suddenly emptied out of fear, and the day my son Travis lost his friend's dad, will be the day that forever changed how they view and trust their world.

(RIGHT) Scallops were poached in a saffron-infused wine sauce, topped with crème fraîche, and served on delicate scallop shells.

(FOLLOWING PAGE LEFT) With a backdrop of vibrant yarn, Cindy Smith offers Martha Giancola, Jean Cheever, Katie Moffit, and Kathleen Gittleman a sampling of the hors d'oeuvres.

(FOLLOWING PAGE RIGHT) Eye-catching tools of the knitting trade fill the walls of the store.

My friend Kathleen is a direct, spirited, incredibly witty, and talented individual. She can make just about anything with a sewing machine, and her intricate and colorful quilts are true works of art. Bored with her lucrative children's clothing business, she started an interior design service. But the design business was lonely. She spent all of her time in her upstairs studio, cutting and sewing. Very much a people person, Kathleen began phasing out the design business and started her quest for something more creative and personally satisfying. She loves to tell the story of her epiphany, which struck her one day when she realized she had just spent an entire afternoon searching for a replacement electric pencil sharpener. To her dismay, with more free time on her hands, she had become the "procurement specialist" for her family. While replenishing supplies was important to the running of her four-person household, this was not how she saw herself or how she wanted to spend the creative years of her life.

(ABOVE AND RIGHT) Flanked by Veronica Szymanski's hand-stitched menu, Chef Ed Batejan's intricate caviar torte was a culinary masterpiece.

In the spring of 2001, Kathleen and I found ourselves at our kids' baseball game, considering what the next chapter of our lives would bring. We talked of opening a store together, but I was more food-oriented, and Kathleen was contemplating a purely artistic venture. Then one sunny day in May, as we sat together again on the Grover Park benches, Kathleen enthusiastically told me she had found what she was meant to do. A trip to a knitting and quilting store in the

Menu

CAVIAR PIE
with Quilted Top

NOODLE WRAPPED SHRIMP
with Spicy Asian Dipping Sauce

POTATO ROQUEFORT PANCAKES
topped with Red Pepper Cream

SAFFRON INFUSED SCALLOPS
with Golden Crème Fraîche

CHIPOTLÉ CHICKEN SATÉS
with Cilantro Dipping Sauce

CONFETTI CORN CAKES
with Roasted Tomato Relish

KATHLEEN'S SPICED PECANS

CHOCOLATE TRUFFLE QUILT CAKE

BUTTON SUGAR COOKIES

nearby town of Pennington had opened her eyes. When she walked into the store, full of baskets of yarn and bolts of quilting fabric, it was kismet. She knew immediately that there would soon be a new knitting, needlepoint, and quilting store in Princeton.

Kathleen began a search for a partner to share in her dream. Quite by accident, she found one while waiting in line for a morning latte at Small World Coffee on Witherspoon Street. Rachel Herr, a

fellow elementary school parent, mother of five, and a bookkeeper by profession but a knitter at heart, admitted to Kathleen that she had always shared the same needlework fantasy. So in the late spring of 2001, the idea for a new business and partnership, which would be called Pins and Needles, was born.

Just when we thought no one was doing crafts anymore, we discovered through Kathleen and Rachel's dream store that we

(PRECEDING PAGE LEFT)
Beth Miro shares knitting
techniques with guests.

(PRECEDING PAGE RIGHT)
Kathleen admires the torte.

(LEFT) Noodle-Wrapped
Shrimp with Thai Chili
Dipping Sauce.

(FOLLOWING PAGE RIGHT)
Spicy Chipotle Chicken
Sates skewered in a zigzag
pattern were served with
a cooling cilantro cream.

secretly still loved needlework. We had been taught as young girls by our grandmothers, mothers, and aunts, but there were still wonderful quilts being stitched, warm sweaters being knitted, and exquisite needlepoint pillows being made. The supplies had changed dramatically; they were now so soft and remarkable in color. But the thought behind the long-cherished projects had stayed the same: the art of giving a handmade gift to someone dear.

Since the closing of Clayton's Yarn Shop on Princeton's Palmer Square, area knitters, needlepointers, and quilters had hoped for a replacement store in the downtown area. Pins and Needles is that and so much more. With an eye for color and a talent for the needle, these two women created a sophisticated, color-intense store that provides crafters, male and female, young and old, with the resources to make sweaters, scarves, pillows, quilts, and even designer shoes, belts, and purses. And if I had been tempted to pick up paintbrushes at Fay Sciarra's art studio, in this overabundance of vivid yarns, intricate needlepoint canvases, and showy quilting fabrics, I gave in and bought a pair of enormous knitting needles and a soft, delicate yarn for a futile attempt by my Austin friend Erin Butler to teach me the simple skill of knitting a winter scarf. Though Erin completed her scarf project—involving a combination of multiple fuzzy expensive yarns—in one quick afternoon, my beginner's try still sits next to the perfectly rolled balls of yarn. I'm not sure if I dropped or picked

up a stitch, but my misshapen scarf is a tedious piece of handiwork that both frustrates and pleases me. The shiny knitting needles sit in a basket beside my comfy bedroom chair, awaiting Erin's return. A knitter I will never be; I'm much too impatient and hopeful for perfection, or at least something that resembles skill.

However, this doesn't stop me from dropping in on Pins and Needles for a wistful look at what could have been. It doesn't stop me from watching knitting maven Beth Miro, without thought, robotically whisking her wooden needles in and out of stunning, colorful, and seemingly complicated strands of yarn, to create an adorable sweet baby hat or a multi-hued, sophisticated sweater that I would have paid hundreds of dollars for in a fashionable boutique. It doesn't keep me from dreaming that someday, perhaps, if I really put my mind to it, I could master this task and appear so at ease with the needle. But a little voice in my head tells me to exit gracefully without a purchase, and to admire the innate skill of others much more talented. Some things are best left to experts.

As I hear the clang of the bell on the door closing behind me, I silently remind myself that we all have our gifts; mine just doesn't involve a knitting needle and yarn, a quilting template or a needlepoint canvas. I think slyly that maybe I'll send them a box of phyllo dough with a simple recipe for fig-and-Gorgonzola-stuffed cheese triangles and see what happens! Oh well—I must resign myself to living out my needlepoint dreams through Kathleen, Rachel, and Beth and numerous other friends who have mastered this frustrating twisting and pulling of yarns into beautiful things. Hopefully, I can hire one of them someday, when my numerous grandchildren come along, to create memorable little sweaters with Winnie-the-Pooh buttons and sweet hats to match—in pink, of course!

tools of the trade

No new store can open without a proper welcome. I promised Kathleen that when Pins and Needles was ready, I would do a party to celebrate the launch of her new business. Originally planned for a Sunday evening in October 2001, the party was postponed. As the calendar turned a year and the store marked its first anniversary alongside September 11, it became apparent that if we were going to celebrate, we would have to pick another time of year. Ultimately, we decided on March, a month of anticipation of warm spring days and new beginnings. More than a hundred friends and family gathered in the small space on Sunday, March 2, 2003, to congratulate Kathleen and Rachel on their year-and-a-half anniversary.

Susan incorporated the elegant turquoise-and-black Pins and Needles shopping bag into the design of our invitation. Susan's mother, Veronica, a successful designer of specialty children's clothing using vintage fabrics, stitched each invitation on a stock card with a fancy zigzag pattern. Buttons were sewn to the invitations to remind guests where they were going, and then the invitations were placed in miniature replicas of the Pins and Needles shopping bags, handles and all. These invitations captured the style of the new store in an entertaining way.

The colors and textures of the hundreds of skeins of yarn and bolts of bright fabric, displayed geometrically in walls of white bins, created a dramatic space for the party. I wanted the food to reflect a few tools of the trade in a clever way. So, of course, I started with dessert first. I asked Ann Bartholomay of Annie B's Confections in Newtown, Pennsylvania, to help design a quilted cake along with button-shaped sugar cookies. We searched through Kathleen's books of quilt patterns and selected "Homeward Bound to Union Square." Annie B's cake designer, Kelly Livesey, spent two days "quilting" the colored fondant and then topped the moist, dense chocolate truffle cake with a blanket of sugar. Set on a stark white worktable in the downstairs yarn room, the cake was the talk of the party. The store's logo colors, soft turquoise and black, were included in both the cake and cookie patterns. Guests were fascinated by the intense color and intricate design of these artistic desserts, and they eagerly awaited the cutting of the cake.

For hors d'oeuvres, we prepared chipotle-breaded chicken sates with a creamy cilantro dip to cool the burn. The result was a spicy,

multidimensional appetizer, which we threaded onto wooden skewers in a zigzag stitch pattern, for serving fun. Shrimp were wrapped with angel-hair pasta, deep-fried, and served with a Thai chili dipping sauce. Scallops were poached in a saffron-infused wine sauce, which resulted in exquisite golden, buttery morsels that melted in the mouth. Miniature Roquefort-cheese potato pancakes were dotted with roasted red pepper and Dijon cream sauce. Kathleen's addictive spicy pecans rounded out the evening's menu.

But the pièce de résistance was the stunning quilted caviar torte, a labor of culinary love. Chef Ed Batejan spent several hours assembling the complicated caviar masterpiece—based on the Lone Star quilt pattern—using Dale's template and much creative patience. The sixteen-inch-square delicious combination of red, black, orange, gold, and green caviar was a visual masterpiece.

(LEFT) A rainbow of threads fills the walls of what was once an art gallery.

(RIGHT) Surrounded by a kaleidoscope of knitting yarn, miniature potato-Roquefort pancakes fill a silver tray.

(FOLLOWING PAGE LEFT) An assortment of snazzy yarns sets this store's selection of needlework supplies apart from the rest.

(FOLLOWING PAGE RIGHT) Buttons and Bows: Annie B's button cookies.

After the quilted cake was cut and the button cookies served, the official opening celebration of Pins and Needles finally became a happy memory. I now can't imagine driving down Chambers Street without checking out the imaginative window displays Kathleen's designer friend Katie Moffit creates for the store each month. Using balls of yarn, knitting needles, needlepoint canvases, or sometimes seasonal bits and pieces, Katie weaves creative messages into each window's-eye view. As I sit in Princeton's rush-hour traffic—ten cars waiting to turn right from Chambers Street onto Nassau Street at five P.M.—I always enjoy taking a peek. No matter what the month, these vignettes remind everyone passing by to slow down and remember what is really important in life: family, home, friends, community. This is especially true of the American-flag-quilt window. Quilted by Kathleen in 2001, and displayed every September as a patriotic reminder and a neighborly memorial, that one can still bring a tear to the eye.

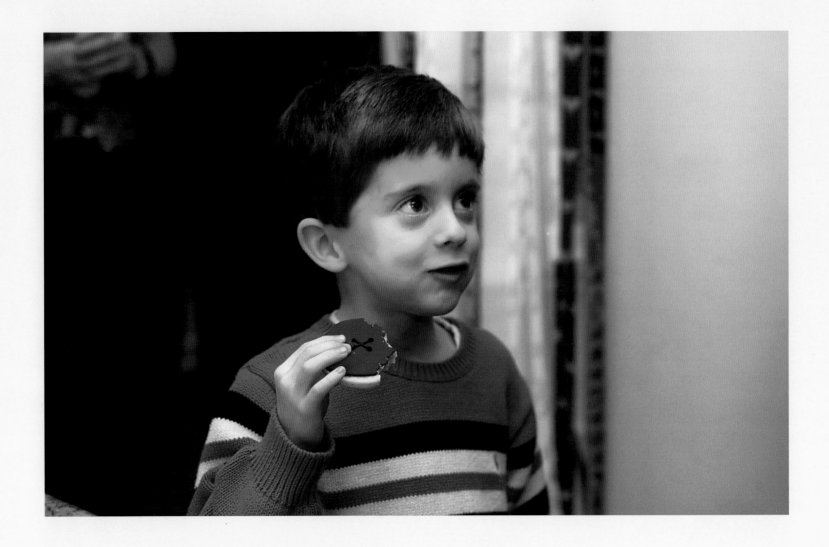

(PRECEDING PAGE LEFT) Annie B's "Homeward Bound to Union Square"
quilt-patterned truffle cake was designed by Kelly Livesey.

(PRECEDING PAGE RIGHT) Finished scarves are designed to tempt
prospective knitters to take a walk on the wild side of their craft.

(ABOVE) After waiting patiently, Kathleen Gittleman's nephew,
Jack, is rewarded with the first button cookie.

(RIGHT) Kathleen's 2001 flag quilt.

a quilted view

What a strange thing is memory, and hope;

one looks backward, the other forward;

one is of today, the other of tomorrow.

— GRANDMA MOSES (1860–1961)

digging dog farm *a gathering of friends*

Fill up a space in a beautiful way.

— GEORGIA O'KEEFFE (1887–1986)

Located just east of Province Line Road, the property is set back about eight hundred feet from Rosedale Road at the end of a gravel driveway. A stone smokehouse stands adjacent to the main house. To the west sits the large barn, a smaller machine barn, a corncrib, and the fenced barnyard, while to the east of the house is the former root cellar, now restored and known affectionately as the Love Shack. Two old chicken coops, power-washed and colorfully painted, serve as changing rooms for the more modern swimming pool. A small pond near the woods completes the in-town country setting.

the old barn

The most impressive building on the property is the massive old barn. Perched on a small incline, the cavernous structure is one of the coolest spots in town during Princeton's hot and humid summer months. When the tall barn doors on each side are slid open, a constant breeze fills the space, creating a virtual wind tunnel. While it originally housed the working farm's horses, cows, and hay, the barn's modern-day view is of the lush and exclusive fairways of the Tournament Players Club of the Jasna Polana golf course, an old leaning corncrib, a small pond surrounded by cattails, and the lower meadow and fenced barnyard, where adopted horses William and Tiger happily graze and run free.

(PRECEDING PAGE) A strong advocate of animal rights, Melita Wright, owner of Digging Dog Farm, opened her heart and home to adopted dog Nellie, a pure mutt, and family pet Bella, a Jack Russell terrier.

(RIGHT) Once part of the Lambert family estate, the 170-year-old barn has been the setting for numerous weddings and special events.

143

Please join me for
CHAMPAGNE IN THE MEADOW
DINNER IN THE BARN

Saturday, the 14th of June
at 7 o'clock in the evening

The Barn at Digging Dog Farm
620 Rosedale Road
Princeton, New Jersey

Please respond
by the 7th of June

dress casual elegant

ANNE REEVES
Princeton, New Jersey 08540

A Gathering of Friends

(ABOVE) Susan chose earthy Italian stock and paired it with shimmery pink paper and silk ribbon to communicate the elegant nature of the barn party.

145

Shhhhh ... this part is a secret!

Write your fondest memory or anecdote or
attach your favorite photograph of Anne
to the enclosed card. Bring it to the party.

We'll share our stories 'round the table
and tuck the cards into
a special memory box for her.

Questions? Call Emily *(not Anne!)*

This event is being photographed for the upcoming book

SACRED SPACES
Princeton Parties, Gatherings & Celebrations

(ABOVE) A coordinating card was enclosed in the invitation asking guests to share their favorite memory of Anne.
The stories were told around the dinner table and the cards presented to Anne as a memento of the evening.

The barn is captivatingly tall, with numerous windows on the second level above the horse stalls. Somehow visitors don't notice the smell of the fresh manure or mind the occasional goat, sheep, chicken, ferret, or dog scurrying around. The place isn't fussy, sanitized, or renovated away from its original charm. The old barn is still rustic, sometimes stinky, and naturally beautiful.

Perhaps that is why brides and grooms flock to the space, wanting to fill it with music, soft lights, and seasonal flowers. Even if a little blowing rain leaks through the weather-beaten walls, wedding guests ignore it and dance the night away. The resulting photographs have a soft, almost aged aura.

Over the years the barn has been filled with bridal parties, graduation celebrations, high school dances, birthday-party paintball-gun escapades, religious pageants, and an assortment of themed public and private school fund-raisers. The barn at Digging Dog Farm is the perfect place to host a gathering of just about any kind.

(PRECEDING PAGE LEFT) The "talented town muse"—Anne Reeves, executive director of the Princeton Arts Council.

(PRECEDING PAGE RIGHT) The twenty-two-foot table was designed to emphasize Anne's personality and well-known flair for spontaneity.

(LEFT TOP) Using treasures from the Winged Pig and Birds of a Feather, Mary Harrison of Euphorbia created a comfortable seating alcove for guests.

(LEFT BOTTOM) Fabric was draped across the wooden support beams and tied with fresh flowers to create an intimate dining space.

a haven for kids and animals

According to the Princeton Historical Society, the farm's 1860 deed lists the original owner simply as T. Baker, followed by W. R. Pease in 1876, and the Lahiere family of Princeton in the early twentieth century. Neighbors fondly remember stopping by the farm to buy fresh eggs from Madame Lahiere. The Lahieres sold the property to Gerard B. Lambert, son of pharmaceutical magnate Jordan Wheat Lambert. Lambert built a sprawling estate on the adjacent property, which he called Albemarle. It included a fifty-two-room main house, which is now home to the American Boychoir School. The Lamberts used 620 Rosedale as servants' quarters and maintained the working farm.

In 1975, Gerald Lambert's widow sold the farm to Dr. Dudley Hawkes, a local orthopedic surgeon, and his wife, Daphne. They raised four children in this ideal country setting. They rode

es, skated on the frozen pond during winter, swam with
ds in the pool in the summer, hid in the barn, and played
an assortment of farm animals. Sadly, the doctor died in a
e crash in the fall of 1985. Daphne sold the farm to Melita
it in 1994.

ng advocate of protecting the environment and rescuing
d or abandoned animals. Melita lives on the farm with

her four children, two horses, numerous egg-laying chickens
a rooster, three cats, and five permanent dogs. The property
was named after Peetie, her now deceased West Highland
white terrier, who had a talent for finding moles hidden deep
within the perennial gardens. The farm has been home to
numerous rescued animals and has served as a foster home
to more than seventy-five abandoned dogs. A volunteer fo
the Trenton Bureau of Animal Control, Melita works with

the Trenton animal shelter to enforce the New Jersey animal cruelty laws. She is a member of the American Society for the Prevention of Cruelty to Animals and an official animal cruelty investigator—badge and all. She is passionate about rescuing animals and finding new, loving families who will welcome them permanently into their lives.

In an environment full of kids, cats, dogs, and an assortment of farm animals, the sometimes timid or fearful wayward dogs get a crash course in socialization, along with a little animal therapy, and soon become adoptable, learning to trust humans again. This time in foster life also provides potential adopting families with the important personality information necessary to select the right dog for their family. Occasionally, an animal arrives at the farm and captures the Wright family's heart so deeply that they just can't let it go. Such was the fate of Izzy and Nellie, two lucky rescued dogs who now call Digging Dog Farm their permanent home.

(LEFT) Anne's daughter, Emily Reeves, left, greets guests enjoying champagne in the meadow.

(RIGHT TOP) Caramelized Shrimp Wrapped in Bacon.

(RIGHT CENTER) Brie Toasts with Caramelized Pepper and Onion Chutney.

(RIGHT BOTTOM) Individual salads of Mesclun Greens with Warmed Goat Cheese and Maple-Dijon Vinaigrette were served on Columbia Depression glass plates, manufactured by the Federal Glass Company between 1938 and 1942.

the talented town muse

Just when you think you must know every person in your small town, a new face appears. Our paths crossed quite serendipitously with that of Anne Reeves. Susan Szymanski is a close family friend; Liz Hosny is Anne's neighbor. Both suggested that Dale and I meet with Anne to discuss including an Arts Council of Princeton event in our book. I had long known of her work as executive director of the Arts Council, but surprisingly, we had never been introduced. As Dale and I sat at Anne's kitchen table, having our third cup of strong coffee and talking about Liz's incredible garden, our book project, and the state of the arts in Princeton, a new friendship was formed. We chatted all morning about Princeton's vast array of talented artists, writers, and architects, and its current and former celebrity residents. Anne shared stories of her dinner with the Robert Oppenheimers, former neighbors on Olden Lane. She talked warmly of her friend the architect Michael Graves's generosity to the Arts Council and our community. She seemed to know just about everyone and everything that was happening creatively in our town.

It also became increasingly clear that through her twenty-one-year involvement in local arts programs, this vibrant, soft-spoken lady from Ohio had become, as her friends call her, the "talented town muse." Before we

(PRECEDING PAGE LEFT) Guest of honor Anne Reeves selected the designs of MacKenzie-Childs scalloped dinner plates for her table.

(PRECEDING PAGE RIGHT) The menu and place cards were printed on fine Italian paper with a deckle edge and incorporated a subtle chicken-wire pattern.

(LEFT) Special Occasions and Queens Street Linens custom-made a 108-inch sheer tablecloth to create the illusion of a single dining table.

(RIGHT) A simple but exquisite first course—Asparagus Gnocchi with Sage and Browned Butter Sauce, garnished with Parmesan-cheese curls and edible flowers.

knew it, instead of planning a fund-raiser, we were focusing on a gathering of Anne's friends to celebrate a lifetime of dedication to our community's arts programs.

During one of our many caffeinated chats over the next few months, Anne told us that one of her favorite sayings was "Now is the time to praise." Feed the soul—let the good times roll—allow individuals to express themselves—connect—organize—build community and preserve traditions—these thoughts poured out when we asked her to describe what the Arts Council programs offered Princeton. According to Anne, the Arts Council welcomes local artists, dancers, musicians, and creative writers of all ages, acting as a conduit for local artisans to establish themselves within the community.

(LEFT) Fragrant lemon-butter
dinner rolls were baked and served
in three-inch terra-cotta pots.

(RIGHT) An elegant main course—
Chef Ed Batejan's Pistachio-Crusted
Halibut with Champagne Cream Sauce,
accompanied by Purple and Gold
Roasted Fingerling Potatoes.

(LEFT) Perfect for any occasion—Annie B's White-Chocolate Satin Tart with Glazed Fresh Raspberries.

Her enthusiasm for this twenty-three-year-old organization, its programs, and the team of supporters who make it all happen was contagious. Anne reveled in the group's successful promotion of town and gown—a mixing of the creative energies of Princeton University and the community, which culminates in an annual street fair called Communiversity. She praised programs such as the Howard B. Waxwood Jr. Scholarship Fund, which enables underprivileged children in the borough and the township to attend the organization's programs and classes. As principal of the former Witherspoon School on Quarry Street, the late Howard Waxwood was one of the developers of the Princeton Plan, which led to the racial integration of Princeton's public schools.

Through its association with and support of such programs as Under Age, Communiversity, Pro Musica, the Shakespeare Festival, and the ever popular Halloween Parade, our community has been served by an outstanding group of individuals who keep the Princeton arts scene vibrant. The Arts Council also hosts a jazz series, poetry readings, and a literary series, and it supports a popular alternative gallery. With such a diverse community, the Arts Council lives a little on the edge in what Anne calls "a Stanley Kunitz kind of way." It embraces everyone with an unwritten mission to "feed the artistic souls and open the hearts and minds of local residents." Education plays a key role, and the Arts Council programs work to bridge the generation gap by serving children, adults, and retired residents.

Melita Wright and Anne Reeves had also never crossed paths, but when we mentioned our desire to use the barn at Digging Dog Farm for the dinner party, Anne immediately recognized the address. It seems that the Reeves and Hawkes families had been good friends and that Anne's son, Neil, had spent many childhood afternoons at the farm. Neil, who now works for Schulte Restorations, had just completed work on a second-floor addition to Melita's farmhouse. While working there, he shared stories of childhood science projects using the barn's fulcrum and told her of his close ties to the Hawkes family. Without question, the barn would be the ideal spot to celebrate Anne's lifelong commitment to the arts.

A phone call confirmed that the Digging Dog space was available in June. When Melita heard the party was for a member of the arts community, she graciously donated the use of the barn for the evening. Anne's daughter, Emily, joined us in the planning. Anne knew only that the guests had been invited for champagne in the meadow and dinner in the barn on Saturday, June 14, 2003. Secretly, we had asked her friends to share a fond memory, a funny anecdote, or a favorite photograph of her at the end of the dinner, as an expression of their relationship with her. These tokens of friendship were occasionally teary, sometimes hilarious, and often inspirational.

champagne in the meadow—dinner in the barn

Petite and sophisticated, Anne is a woman with a creative sense of style, someone who loves the unusual and unexpected about life. When she entertains at home, she fills her dining room table with whatever appeals to her from along the roadside or in her backyard, whether it's a budding springtime tree branch, a bundle of just-cut summer daisies, or scattered autumn leaves and a collection of oddly shaped gourds.

When you first meet Anne, you might be tempted to select a soft pink for her table, but further into your acquaintance, you would definitely add accents of fuchsia with bursts of sunny yellow. The setting for the twenty-two-foot-table needed to emphasize her strong but generous personality and that daring flair for spontaneity we had heard so much about. We asked Anne to select a table design preference: bold hand-painted pottery plates and an unusual combination of stemware, or an antique china pattern complemented by pieces of vintage Depression glass. Her selection was instantaneous—the wild and crazy combinations offered by the MacKenzie-Childs pottery.

To complete the table, we combined patterned MacKenzie-Childs scalloped chargers with inexpensive salad plates in harmonizing colors from a local department store. Dessert would be served on clear 1930s pressed-glass plates in the Columbia pattern. To achieve the illusion of a continuous dinner table, Claudia Himes of Special Occasions and Queens Street Linens in Lancaster, Pennsylvania, custom-made a floor-length 108-inch sheer lattice-patterned table topper, which covered several soft mint-green tablecloths. The completed table for twenty-four was striking.

Using borrowed treasures from the Winged Pig in the Princeton Shopping Center, along with numerous private pieces, Mary Harrison of Euphorbia in Lawrenceville created a cozy indoor alcove for guests to sit and relax during cocktails. She also emphasized the adjacent dining space by draping fabric across the support beams. Karen Graves of Plant Profiles lit the barn's darkest corners with twinkling trees. Candles were submerged in tall glass urns filled halfway with water and floating summer flowers. Adriene Presti of Dahlia's Floral Concepts in Pennington placed numerous small vases of flowers down the center of the long table. Spotlights were directed upward to accent the height and beauty of the wooden ceiling and to illuminate the whimsical cardboard full moon attached to the wall during a previous year's Oktoberfest celebration. The surprise of the evening—if only we had been clever enough to plan this—was the real full moon rising unexpectedly in the evening sky, tossing moonlight through cracks in the barn walls onto the candlelit table.

(RIGHT) A view from
the barn loft.

(LEFT) The surprise of
the evening—
a moonlit table.

(FOLLOWING PAGE RIGHT)
The corncrib aglow.

With no kitchen facilities near the barn, preparation of the food was a challenge, but we were fortunate to have the machine barn close by, with electricity and a roof. After power-washing the floor, we converted the barn to a catering kitchen with numerous worktables, a professional-sized gas range and oven, and access to a refrigerated truck. Weather permitting, we would offer hors d'oeuvres and champagne in the meadow and invite guests to sit for their first course. After that, multiple hands would be needed to deliver four courses across the lawn.

Chef Ed Batejan and I were excited about cooking for a smaller guest list, which would allow us to do something more creative with each course. Annie B had been waiting for the perfect occasion to offer her White Chocolate Satin Tart, floating in a luscious pool of raspberry coulis, so dessert was easily decided. We asked our guest of honor to politely poll her friends to see whether fish could be an option for the main course. Everyone enjoyed seafood, so we decided on halibut, a succulent and moist fish that's perfect for a dinner party; with Ed's pistachio-nut crust and a champagne cream sauce, it was an elegant main course. Sides of roasted baby vegetables and colorful red and yellow fingerling potatoes rounded out the plate. Mesclun salad greens topped with warm goat-cheese rounds and dressed with a maple-syrup-based vinaigrette preceded the main course. Lemon-crusted dinner rolls baked in three-inch terra-cotta pots added an element of whimsy.

It was the first course, our simplest dish, that stole the show. Fresh asparagus-filled gnocchi were tossed with a browned butter, fresh sage, and lemon sauce and topped with Parmesan-cheese curls and lemon zest. I can still remember the scent of this mouth-watering dish being carried barn-to-barn, filling the night air.

As the evening drew to a close and stories, fond memories, and funny photographs were shared with Anne and her guests, Melita, Dale, and I sat by the fire pit in the meadow and looked up at the barn, glowing against the evening sky. We heard laughter and murmuring, followed by the clinking of glasses. As guests strolled down to the meadow to say their goodbyes, Anne emerged from the barn with her children by her side. With a radiant smile, she told us that "this was the type of evening we all should have at least once in our lives. Those who are lucky enough to enjoy the moment while still alive on this earth are truly blessed." No better thank-you could have been offered to the tired workers who would spend the next few hours returning the barn to its natural state.

The true harvest of my daily life is somewhat as intangible and indescribable as the tints of morning or evening. It is a little star-dust caught, a segment of the rainbow which I have clutched.

— HENRY DAVID THOREAU (1817–1862)

164

living at 620 Rosedale Road, I was glad to hear that this prized piece of farmland, once lovingly called Digging Dog Farm, will remain an important piece of Princeton Township's charm, history, and natural appeal.

As I sip morning coffee in my robe on our back terrace, I can witness the power of preservation at close range. My breakfast view now includes a small portion of the recently preserved Greenway Meadows Park on Rosedale Road. Princeton Township is fortunate to have secured these sixty acres for public use through public funding and contributions made by private donors. Once home to General Robert Wood Johnson and previously a part of Edgerstoune Farm and the 273-acre Archibald Russell estate, the 1800s and early 1900s. Soon, a little farther down this road, the new owners of 620 Rosedale Road, once part of the Lambert estate, will look out their barn doors and catch a glimpse of the full moon that bursts from beneath the rolling fairway greens of Jasna Polana and glides over the wooded fields. The thought of another small portion of our town's land remaining much as it was a century ago pleases the romantic in me. The shared experience of celebrating in a space alive with local history will establish a permanent bond to our past and unite us to each generation that follows.

And hopefully, like Madame Lahiere and Melita, the new owners will continue to offer fresh farm eggs to grateful friends and neighbors.

the hesters' garden *east meets west*

O Jizo san
Save the children.
Bring love, blessings, and peace.

— JAN CHOZEN BAYS (1945–)

The loss of a child is an incomprehensible tragedy that forever alters the focus of a parent's life. For Nancy and Jim Chuda, the memory of their five-year-old daughter, Colette, who died in 1991 of Wilm's tumor, a nonhereditary cancer, was the impetus to question how exposure to toxins in daily environments can harm children. Desperate to find an answer to what triggered their daughter's cancer, they found there was little research on the link between maternal exposure to pesticides and early-childhood cancers. Together with Nancy's best friend and Colette's godmother, singer Olivia Newton-John, in 1991, they established the Colette Chuda Environmental Fund (CCEF), a nonprofit organization based in California, to research how environmental toxins affect children's health.

(PRECEDING PAGE) The Hesters purchased the urn and the lions that accent the side garden wall in Little Venice in West London, England. They were used in the movie *101 Dalmations*.

(LEFT) Jim Hester's serious lifetime hobby of portrait painting has become a second career, but his favorite model is Janet, his wife of over fifty years.

(RIGHT) A rear view: Woodrow Wilson lived in the Cleveland Lane house when he was governor of New Jersey.

CCEF launched the Children's Health and Environmental Coalition (CHEC) in 1992 to inform parents about preventable health and development problems caused by exposures to sometimes hidden toxic substances within our homes, schools, and communities. CHEC would ultimately ask the United States Congress to seek ways to shield children from common household chemicals and toxins. With the support of high-profile board members such as Dr. Philip J. Landrigan of the Mount Sinai School of Medicine, spokespersons Olivia Newton-John and actress Kelly Preston, and well-known environmental activist Erin Brockovich, the group captured national media attention in 2001 as it brought its science-based environmental health information to policy makers and the public, and offered safer alternatives. Its *First Steps* video and environmental childproofing campaign will reach more than four million pregnant women annually with a strong prevention message.

A puzzle of well-structured but intimate spaces, each outdoor room was a reflection of natural beauty where a visitor could leave behind the stress of everyday life. From the mass of springtime bluebells beneath the weeping cherry trees to an enchanting stone statue of a gazing child, the garden symbolized the Japanese philosophy of the spiritual journey of life amid serene views that changed with each passing step. With subtle Japanese influences of water, stone, and plants, the garden was a place of peace and healing: a pocket of grace hidden behind a simple brown wooden gate, surrounded by walls of swaying bamboo stalks, and layered with a soft carpet of evergreen. A small stone jizo statue representing Bodhisattva—guardian of travelers and protector of women and small children—quietly stood guard. This would be the ideal setting to reflect on the brief life of Colette Chuda and, with a sense of hope and responsibility, to reinforce CHEC's message that by protecting our environment, we also protect our children.

When I mentioned this particular address to several friends, I learned that it had quite a following among gardening enthusiasts. The Hesters' home had often been included on Garden Club of America and Philadelphia Garden Club tours but was hidden from everyday view behind a tall fence. The meticulously planted front yard hinted at the splendid space on the other side of the back gate, but from the sidewalks of Cleveland Lane, the interior gardens remained a mystery.

(LEFT) *Gazer*, circa 1950, surrounded by pink New Dawn climbing roses.
The stone sculpture was created by Anne Jaggard Kopper, born in 1893;
she had six children and twenty-two grandchildren, who were often her subjects.

(FOLLOWING PAGE RIGHT) Tree peony.

The backyard of this prominent Tudor-style house, built in 1907 by the artist Parker Mann, preserved the work of two master landscape artists, Robert Zion and Yuji Yoshimura. Known for his design of Liberty State Park and Riverfront Park in Cincinnati, Robert Zion planned the Hesters' 1981 redesign of their Princeton garden. The Japanese garden on the upper level was created and maintained by the late Yuji Yoshimura, one of the best-known bonsai artists in the world.

The Hesters purchased the house in 1964, when Jim was president of New York University. In 1975 he resigned from the university to serve as the first rector of the United Nations University in Tokyo. It was during their five years in Japan that he and Janet became captivated with the art of Japanese landscapes. The New York Botanical Garden lured Jim back to the States to serve as their director from 1980 to 1989, and it was there that he became associated with Yuji Yoshimura, who taught at the

According to Janet, Jim came home from work one day and told her that if he was going to direct such prestigious gardens they should probably have a nice garden in Princeton. While previous owners had landscaped with traditional perennial beds, the Hesters decided to bring an Eastern influence to their surroundings. The combination of an appreciation for Japanese-style landscapes, Jim's newest career challenge and a deep sensitivity to the environment resulted in the creation of this magnificent natural space.

When Dale and I first met the Hesters, they were planning their fiftieth wedding anniversary celebration, a small recital for the Princeton Symphony Orchestra, and the annual Reunions Weekend at Princeton University. It was apparent that they were a couple used to large-scale entertaining. They are the parents of three grown daughters and the wedding of their second daughter, Meg Giroux, was held at the New York Botanical Gardens and featured in

Design the garden so that its beauty accords with the site and responds to the passage of time as sensitively as do leaves in a whispering breeze, with nothing clumsy or coarse about it. The result must be fascinating in a quiet, graceful way.

—ILLUSTRATIONS FOR DESIGNING
MOUNTAIN, WATER, AND HILLSIDE FIELD LANDSCAPES (1466)

Gracious and welcoming, Janet offered us a brief tour of their historic home before we viewed the garden. Once the residence of Woodrow Wilson when he was governor of New Jersey, the house on Cleveland Lane is now filled with a lifetime of personal collections and numerous portraits of family members, past and present. A photograph of Woodrow Wilson, taken on his way from the house to Washington, D.C., for his presidential inauguration, hangs by the living room wet bar. Containers filled with morning flowers dot antique tabletops throughout the first floor. The elegant but comfortable home was welcoming—full of music, art, and book collections, along with Japanese accents that complemented rather than competing with the traditional decor.

As Janet guided us through the traditional butler's pantry and into the kitchen, my cook's eye immediately went to the pair of 1940s Hardwick gas stoves. Janet said they had been in the kitchen when they bought the house and still worked beautifully. With the flick of a switch, the space above the old stove clocks illuminated, and the freestanding ovens became bold works of kitchen art. While the rest of Janet's kitchen had been updated, I admired her for preserving the vintage stoves as a focal point, and I was charmed by the fact that they were now being used to prepare meals for a couple celebrating their fiftieth wedding anniversary.

Meigakure

Perhaps the most important concept of traditional Japanese gardens, the quality of remaining hidden from ordinary view.

As we passed through the breezeway, we heard soft koto music, and Jim's studio came into view. Designed by local architect Glen Fries, the room was encased in floor-to-ceiling glass walls and ceiling skylights. Natural light filled the space. Easels held artworks in progress, and containers of paints and brushes filled side tables. Walls in the adjacent second studio were covered with photographs of completed commissions. I recognized a portrait of Puddie's youngest daughter, Payson. Much like Fay Sciarra's studio, the room emanated a sense of passion and deep commitment. It was clear that Jim took to heart the challenge of capturing an individual's essence.

What was a serious lifetime hobby had, over time, become a new career. This studio had been added on to the almost century-old house at a time when the Hesters' children had long since left for marriages, careers, and families of their own, and at a point when most careers were exchanged for retirement, and large family homes replaced by easy-to-maintain condos. As I looked at the faces on the walls, I thought that Jim's portraits offered an unspoken message—to pursue and cultivate the earliest of youthful dreams and embrace rather than fear the gift of growing older, welcoming the challenges that push us forward and allow us to view the world in a wiser light.

the garden

As we looked through the wall of studio windows, the powerful natural view of the connected garden captured and held our attention. A few steps down lay a magnificent Japanese-inspired landscape. After many seasons of viewing the space, Jim and Janet knew its peak moments, and they began excitedly describing how thousands of bluebells, which I assumed were similar to my favored Texas bluebonnets, would appear in mid-May under the weeping cherry trees. It was difficult to remember, as we walked into the garden, that we were surrounded on all sides by traditional Princeton backyards.

Dale and I were left to explore the numerous pathways that lined the garden. As I passed the reflecting pool and walked toward the house, I caught a glimpse of an enchanting space, identified only by a small arch filled with a budding pink New Dawn climbing rose. Set behind a semicircular wall in the center of the garden, almost hidden from view by intricately woven ivy tendrils and profuse lilac bushes, was a statue of a gazing child holding a small bowl. The child's eyes looked away from visitors. A stone bench and a time-worn brick walkway invited the guest to enter and rest for a while. This haunting statue epitomized the mystery of the garden, and it became the focal point of our CHEC invitation.

(LEFT, RIGHT TOP, RIGHT BOTTOM) A touch of springtime in the Hesters' garden.

(RIGHT CENTER) Nancy Chuda and Puddie Sword.

the koto

THE KOTO IS A THIRTEEN-STRINGED WOODEN INSTRUMENT MEASURING ALMOST SEVEN FEET LONG. THE PITCH IS ADJUSTED WITH MOVABLE BRIDGES PLACED UNDER EACH STRING. IT IS PLAYED WITH PICKS, CALLED *TSUME*, SIMILAR TO THOSE USED WITH A GUITAR. THE NAMES FOR PARTS OF A KOTO WERE DERIVED FROM THE IMAGE OF A DRAGON STRETCHED OUT ALONG THE GROUND. THE BODY IS CALLED THE *RYUKO* (DRAGON'S BACK). THE *JI* (BRIDGES) ARE SUPPORTS THAT SLIDE UP AND DOWN THE INSTRUMENT TO ADJUST THE SOUND. THE *TSUME* (CLAWS) ARE WORN ON THREE FINGERS (INDEX, MIDDLE, AND THUMB OF THE RIGHT HAND), AND THE STRINGS ARE PLUCKED WITH THEM. THE KOTO DATES FROM THE FIFTH TO THE THIRD CENTURY B.C. IN CHINA. IT ORIGINALLY HAD ONLY FIVE STRINGS. THE THIRTEEN-STRING KOTO WAS CARRIED TO JAPAN DURING THE NARA PERIOD (710–794).

(LEFT TOP) The Tea Ladies, front to back, Kimiko Otsuka, Yoshiko Okuda, Eri Ninomiya, Mineko Hirayama, and Satomi Kobayashi. The Princeton Tea Ladies are a group of women from Japan who meet once a month to share the ancient art of the tea ceremony.

(LEFT BOTTOM) Masayo Ishigure entertained guests with her traditional koto music.

the art of tea

THE JAPANESE TEA CEREMONY CAPTURES ALL THE ELEMENTS OF JAPANESE PHILOSOPHY AND ARTISTIC BEAUTY AND INTERWEAVES FOUR PRINCIPLES: HARMONY WITH PEOPLE AND NATURE; RESPECT FOR OTHERS; PURITY OF HEART AND MIND; AND TRANQUILITY. IT GREW FROM THE CUSTOM OF ZEN BUDDHIST MONKS DRINKING TEA FROM A SINGLE BRONZE BOWL IN FRONT OF A STATUE OF THEIR FOUNDER, BUDHIDHARMA, DURING THE ACT OF WORSHIP. OVER THE CENTURIES, RITUALS DEVELOPED AROUND THE RELIGIOUS SIGNIFICANCE AND THE USE AND APPRECIATION OF THE UTENSILS USED TO PREPARE AND SERVE TEA. BECOMING A TRUE TEA MASTER IS A LIFETIME'S WORK, AND THE TRAINING PROCESS IS NEVER REALLY COMPLETED. EACH TEA OCCASION LINKS THE PEOPLE TAKING PART TO A CONTINUOUS CHAIN OF 885 YEARS OF TEA HISTORY.

(PRECEDING PAGE RIGHT TOP) Crunchy Shrimp Tempura prepared by Mr. Choi of the Nassau Bagel and Sushi Company.

(PRECEDING PAGE RIGHT BOTTOM) Glazed Yellowfin Tuna Bites in Wonton Cups.

(LEFT) Chicken Yakitori.

(RIGHT) Sesame Salmon Squares with Lemon Miso Sauce.

(FOLLOWING PAGE LEFT TOP) Carrot and Ginger Pancakes with Tamari Chili Sauce.

(FOLLOWING PAGE LEFT BOTTOM) Gingered Pork and Cabbage Inari Pockets.

(FOLLOWING PAGE RIGHT) A budding rhododenron.

Months later, after the invitations had been mailed, I asked Janet to tell me the story behind the statue. It was just as perfect as the setting. She had admired a similar one while visiting a friend's home in Connecticut. As a surprise, her mother had one made for their twenty-fifth wedding-anniversary gift. Twenty-five years later, as they celebrated their fiftieth anniversary, the statue still held a place of honor in the garden.

never count on the weather

The first rule for an outside party is to assume the weather will not cooperate. While a Japanese garden might be mystical in a soft summer rain, guests don't usually want to stroll through wet grass with umbrellas and cocktails in hand. After weeks of endless rain, the ground was already soggy, so we called Brian Richardson at L&A Tents and reserved a tent, just in case. The party started at five P.M., so our decision deadline was noon.

Of course, the chance of afternoon thundershowers continued to be 50 percent. While Janet offered to move the entire party inside, the thought of a hundred pairs of wet shoes on her beautiful floors and rugs made us cringe. In the end, the tent had to go up. We set the sushi bar under the covered porch and placed the tent as close to the house deck as possible. At least the remainder of the garden would appear untouched.

At party time, the sun occasionally peeked through the heavy clouds, the humidity level dropped, and the torrential rains held off until the following day. Our linen-covered tables and garden chairs sank deeper into the rain-soaked lawn, but guests didn't seem to notice; most moved out from under the tent to the small round tables set next to the reflecting pool. Here they enjoyed Masayo Ishigure's traditional koto music along with the lush view. A few guests rocked on the charming Old Charleston joggling board (a sixteen-foot-long bouncing bench that often graces porches and gardens of the Deep South), which somehow looked at home in this setting. Even our visiting Tea Ladies—a group of women who gather in Princeton monthly to practice the art of the Japanese tea ceremony dressed in traditional kimonos—ventured onto a garden path for a group photograph.

think globally, act locally

The food possibilities for this party were exciting, and the challenge of preparing them organically was an education. Through their association with CHEC, several organic farming companies—such as Earthbound Farms, Eden Farms, and Santa Cruz Organic—donated ingredients. We incorporated traditional ingredients, like ginger, miso, sesame, soy sauce, mirin, and rice vinegar, and the menu included many elements of the Japanese table: sushi, chicken yakitori, shrimp tempura, and tofu. With little knowledge of how to prepare these traditional recipes, I spent hours researching cookbooks, visiting local restaurants, and talking

to sushi chefs. Most recipes had an interesting myth or cultural ritual associated with them.

The most fascinating recipe lore was based on fried bean curd, the main ingredient for the Inari Pork and Cabbage Pockets. Chef Ed Batejan suggested that we include his version of fried tofu pockets stuffed with succulent soy-and-ginger-flavored pork. Also called *aburage* or *koage*, these teriyaki-seasoned deep-fried bean-curd pockets are most often filled with vinegared rice to make a form of sushi called inari-zushi, which is offered to the god at shrines throughout Japan. Inari is one of the most mysterious deities of the Shinto religion, in which all things, including inanimate objects and forces of nature, have a soul. Inari, the Japanese god of food or the goddess of rice, is both male and female and symbolizes prosperity and friendship. As a

(LEFT TOP, LEFT BOTTOM)
CHEC spokesperson
Olivia Newton-John and
her business partner,
Pat Farrar, donated their
Australian Koala Blue
wines for the event.

(RIGHT) Annie B's Raspberry-
Almond Tea Cakes and
the garden's stone jizo,
representing Bodhisattva—
guardian of travelers and
protector of women and
small children.

(FOLLOWING PAGE LEFT)
Haiku cookies:
In a dream
My daughter lifts a melon
To her soft cheek
—KOBAYASHI ISSA (1763–1827)

(FOLLOWING PAGE RIGHT)
Annie B's sweet interpretation
of the Japanese motif on
Susan's invitation design.

goddess, Inari is depicted either as a woman with long, flowing hair carrying two sheaves of rice, or as a long-haired woman riding a white fox. Inari may also appear as an old man with a long beard. I found the symbolism, celebrating friendship and prosperity, both male and female, a perfect fit for the CHEC menu.

In addition to the more traditional Japanese foods, we added ginger-carrot-parsnip pancakes with tamari-chili dipping sauce and delicate endive spears filled with a savory herb cheese and plum salsa, and topped with organic edible flowers. Throughout this research period, my sons became addicted to sushi, sashimi, yakitori, tempura, and most of all, the hot and spicy Sriracha hot sauce that is a staple on most Japanese tables. After tasting Chef Choi's crunchy shrimp tempura at the Nassau Bagel and Sushi Company on Nassau Street, Travis even overcame his aversion to shrimp. After my numerous tasting trips, Chef Choi finally took pity on me and invited me into his kitchen, where he demonstrated the secret to his crisp tempura coating, called *koromo*.

I decided the dessert had to be something light and delicate but as dramatic as the hors d'oeuvres. While Annie B and I discussed various cookies, bars, and tea cakes one morning at the local ice-skating rink, Vicki Helgenberg, Anne's children's skating coach, offered us a fresh-baked cookie. The light and pleasing oatmeal and lemon were the perfect combination of flavors for a garden party; Vicki generously offered to share her recipe. With one cookie down, we somehow—and no one can quite seem to remember who suggested the task—decided it would be fun to write the invitation's haiku kanji symbols on individual sugar cookies. The research for this project turned out to be immensely time-consuming, as the reverse translation—from English back to Japanese—was difficult to find. Everyone we asked had a different idea of the correct kanji. But thanks to Sahoko Okabyhasi, a Japanese-language teacher at the Lawrenceville School, we at last came upon what we hoped would be an acceptable translation, and Caroline Loevner wrote it for us. Once again, the talented designers Kelly Livesey and Doria Lenicky at Annie B's Confections came through, creating striking black-and-white haiku cookies.

Dozens of cookies later, this intriguing but edible translation was presented on a woven bamboo mat for guests to admire and enjoy. Delicate raspberry-and-almond tea cakes with organic violets and Asian spice

(LEFT) The stone elephant from Japan, circa 1907, was inherited by Janet from her godmother.

(RIGHT TOP) Photographer Ricardo Barros captured the beauty of a single spring bluebell—*Endymion hispanicus*—in a sea of thousands. This brilliant blue flower is said to represent lasting love and constancy. They are so popular throughout England that they are considered the national flower.

(RIGHT BOTTOM) Raspberry Almond Tea Cakes with a touch of blue.

(FOLLOWING PAGE LEFT) The powerful mature stalks of the giant bamboo wall, from a frozen winter state to soft springtime buds, provide a barrier from neighboring yards and visually fence in the dramatic aura of the garden's seasons.

(FOLLOWING PAGE RIGHT) The *Gazer* on a winter day.

okies completed the dessert table. We ...ped our menu and the special setting ...ould emphasize the connection we all ...ve to nature and the importance of ...eserving the delicate balance between ...an and his environment.

...ivia Newton-John donated her wines, ...ala Blue Australian Shiraz 2001 and ...ala Blue Australian Chardonnay ...01. The striking blue and red bottles ...corated the bar table. Eric Roberts of ...rdinière Florals filled hollow bamboo ...alks with soft pink peonies and ...licate sprigs of spring bamboo from ...e Hesters' garden. Table linens were ...mple, in soft muted colors.

...embers of the Princeton community ...tened attentively to Nancy Chuda's ...ory of her daughter Colette's illness ...d the effort to inform other parents of ...e dangers of environmental toxins. Dr. ...ilip Landrigan spoke about ongoing ...search linking maternal exposure. ...HEC had a successful introduction ...Princeton, and for a second time

essential

PERHAPS THE MOST
IMPORTANT CONCEPT O[F]
TRADITIONAL JAPANESE
GARDENS, *MEIGAKURE* IS
THE QUALITY OF
REMAINING HIDDEN
FROM ORDINARY VIEW.
EACH FEATURE OF THE
GARDEN APPEARS FROM
PARTIAL CONCEALMENT,
CREATING A PROFOUND
SENSE OF MYSTERY AND
ENCOURAGING VISITORS
TO CONTINUE THEIR
JOURNEY. THE THREE
ESSENTIAL ELEMENTS OF
JAPANESE GARDENING
ARE WATER, FOR ITS
SOOTHING AND
REFLECTIVE QUALITIES;
ROCK, FOR ITS SENSE
OF PERMANENCE; AND
PLANTS, FOR THEIR
TEXTURES AND SHADES
OF GREEN.

in the garden, the East–West connection was made.

The best part of any party is that moment when you can truly relax and watch your guests enjoy the setting that was created in their honor. As dessert was served, Dale, Susan, and I sat down by the circular reflecting pool to listen to Masayo Ishigure's koto music. As I looked back toward the house and upper garden and saw tables filled with chatting friends and neighbors, most nibbling on one of our haiku cookies, I thought that perhaps, for that evening, we had achieved what the Japanese call *Tei En* or *niwa sono*—the balance between nature and man-made beauty.

in her backyard *the last rose of summer*

In joy or sadness, flowers are our constant friends.

—KOZUKO OKAKURA (1862–1913)

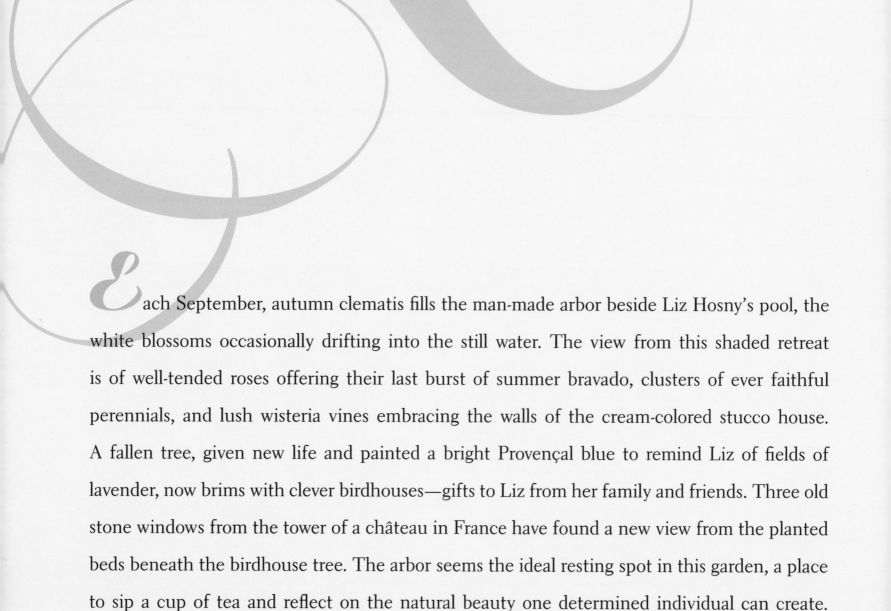

*E*ach September, autumn clematis fills the man-made arbor beside Liz Hosny's pool, the white blossoms occasionally drifting into the still water. The view from this shaded retreat is of well-tended roses offering their last burst of summer bravado, clusters of ever faithful perennials, and lush wisteria vines embracing the walls of the cream-colored stucco house. A fallen tree, given new life and painted a bright Provençal blue to remind Liz of fields of lavender, now brims with clever birdhouses—gifts to Liz from her family and friends. Three old stone windows from the tower of a château in France have found a new view from the planted beds beneath the birdhouse tree. The arbor seems the ideal resting spot in this garden, a place to sip a cup of tea and reflect on the natural beauty one determined individual can create.

(RIGHT) A touch of
pink champagne.

(LEFT) Janet Lasley
and Liz Hosny.

(FOLLOWING PAGE RIGHT)
The clematis-covered
arbor is a quiet place
to reflect on the beauty
of Liz's garden.

While contemplating this pleasant setting shortly after September 11, 2001, Janet Lasley decided that her friend Liz was being selfish with her peaceful retreat. Janet walked into the kitchen she had helped renovate and instructed Liz to share her garden. Never one to ignore a good friend's advice, and a believer in an open-door policy, Liz decided a week later as she walked through her garden, noticing her Peace rose in bloom, that she would do just that. She opened her garden gate and invited not only friends and neighbors but the entire Princeton community to come and sit for a few minutes, an hour, or even the whole day. On September 28, 2001, a glorious fall day, Liz welcomed more than a hundred friends, acquaintances, and community leaders. With the help of a few good neighbors and the YWCA Newcomers Club, she offered simple refreshments—fruits, muffins, sandwiches, tea, and coffee. A small basket was set next to the garden gate for donations to the United Way September 11 Fund.

The casual invitation went out via e-mail, telephone, word of mouth, and local newspapers. Guests from all over town drifted in and out. Some brought bag lunches and came on their lunch hour. Others showed up for morning coffee and stayed for afternoon tea. This uncomplicated gesture of goodwill and caring raised over five thousand dollars for victims' families. After weeks of funerals and memorial services, this day was about neighborly companionship and a small step toward healing a deep communal wound. Liz Hosny opened her garden for quiet reflection and a cup of tea. Who could have asked for anything more?

home at last

Built by Frank H. Constant, once a professor of engineering at Princeton University, and his wife, Annette, Liz's 1915 Colonial home on Battle Road is known as the Constant House. It was in total disrepair in 1995 when Realtor Maggie Hill first showed it to Liz and her husband, Zaki, who were planning to settle in Princeton after twenty years of international corporate travel. Despite the house's condition, which they describe as an uninsurable ruin, the couple felt an immediate *coup de foudre*— love at first sight—when they saw it. The plane-tree-lined street reminded them of their beloved Provence, and during the house tour, Zaki had found numerous maps of his favorite cities in France—Arles, Avignon, and the Pont du Gard—dating from the 1950s. When he saw a guidebook to Oslo, Norway, where he was currently living, he decided the house had to be theirs.

On a snowy afternoon in November 1995, Liz and Zaki hired Lasley Construction and Brahaney Architectural Associates to renovate and modernize the house, adding, among other things, a large kitchen and family room and an updated master bedroom suite. Two days later, after reviewing preliminary architectural drawings, the Hosnys returned to Brussels, entrusting the husband-and-wife team of Janet Lasley and Marc Brahaney with the nine-month job. After numerous transatlantic faxes and phone calls, Liz and Zaki returned in August to a completed interior renovation. The garden was, however, another story.

When you have lived abroad in leased houses much of your adult life, the terms "home" and "garden" must be flexible. As Liz says, "To itinerants like us, home is simply where we are!" Prior to moving to Princeton, Liz and Zaki had lived in seven countries, and shared six houses and one apartment, and had two children. It wasn't until they purchased their first home in New Zealand that Liz began seriously flirting with the idea of tending her own plot of land.

The daughter of two dedicated English gardeners, Liz grew up on a farm in East Anglia, northeast of London. She lived in a five-hundred-year-old house and celebrated the arrival of indoor plumbing and electricity when it came to the village. As a child, Liz often had difficulty accepting her parents' devotion to their four acres of manicured gardens and farm. She resented the fact that her family could never travel, lest the flowers be left unattended; frustrated, she swore she would never devote herself to a plot of dirt and seeds with such fervor—what nonsense! The daily commitment of watering, pruning, and fertilizing necessary to maintain the ideal English garden seemed, to Liz, total rubbish.

But when an empty acre of American soil presented itself, Liz succumbed to her heritage and became a gardener. Down on her knees she went, with trowel and flats of perennials in hand. With a blank canvas and the vision and patience of landscape designer Dick Karkalits, Liz began her first attempt to build a garden.

(ABOVE) Garden sculpture representing Liz and Zaki's daughter, Laura.

Liz's commitment to a comfortable home and an inviting garden has resulted in an environment where her friends feel comfortable enough to just stop by and sit for a while at her kitchen counter, sometimes even when she's not home. If it's a sunny spring, summer, or autumn afternoon, they always know where to find her: in the garden, digging, planting, or feeding her plants. This space is not just taken care of; it is nurtured. In transforming this corner of Princeton, Liz has filled each nook and cranny with a touch of England, France, Belgium, New Zealand, and New Jersey.

In a gesture of her fondness for the gardens of England, Beatrix took ivy cuttings from the gardens of Martin Luther at Wittenburg, Oxford, and Cambridge universities and placed them in the Wyman House garden, residence of the dean of the Graduate College. Massed plantings of dogwoods, sugar maples, beech, sweet gum, and tulip poplars created soothing vistas across the campus for studious eyes to enjoy. "We all know that education is by no means a mere matter of books, and that the aesthetic environment contributes as much to growth as facts assembled from a printed page," Beatrix Farrand wrote in the *Princeton Alumni Weekly*, June 6, 1926.

After her parents divorced, Beatrix was guided by her paternal aunt, novelist Edith Wharton—also a passionate gardener, and an arbiter of taste in American society during the Gilded Age (1865–1929). Beatrix grew up in the privileged world of New York society, and her mother's salon was often filled with notable writers such as Henry James, who nicknamed Beatrix "Trix." During the era of the country estate (the late nineteenth and early twentieth centuries), landscape architects were in great demand and received substantial commissions to design country estate gardens. After introductions by Aunt Edith to prominent members of New York society, Beatrix was hired to design gardens for clients such as John D. Rockefeller and Mrs. Henry Cabot Lodge.

The only female among the founders of the American Society of Landscape Architects, Beatrix became a role model for other women of her generation. Her only formal training began when she was twenty, with an apprenticeship to Charles Sprague Sargent, dean of American horticulture and the founder and first director of Harvard University's Arnold Arboretum. In 1913, Mrs. Woodrow Wilson invited Beatrix to design the East Garden of the White House. Beatrix would also aid in the design of the West Garden, transform the grounds at Yale University, and design library grounds for the J. Pierpont Morgan Library in New York and the Huntington Library in California.

Beatrix maintained long-term relationships with most of her clients, but she was especially close to diplomat Robert Woods Bliss and his wife, Mildred. Their estate, Dumbarton Oaks, was set on fifty-three acres in the Georgetown section of Washington, D.C. Dumbarton Oaks became Beatrix's *chef d'oeuvre*—the most important design of her lifetime. A mixture of traditional English, French, and Italian styles, its highlights included a rose garden, an English country garden, and an orangery.

After dedicating herself to these gardens for almost twenty years, Beatrix agreed to write her famous *Plant Book* in 1941, at almost seventy years old. This detailed guide to the garden's design, maintenance, and preservation is now considered an important document in the history of the development of landscape architecture in twentieth-century America.

> *"Her love of beauty and order is everywhere visible in what she planted for our delight."*
>
> —INSCRIPTION FROM THE IVY-SHADED
> CURVED BENCH INSTALLED
> IN BEATRIX FARRAND'S HONOR
> NEXT TO THE PRINCETON UNIVERSITY CHAPEL

the tower

To view Beatrix's work on the Princeton campus, you must first pass through the formidable entrance to the Graduate College, a series of residence and dining halls designed to isolate graduate students from the distractions of undergraduate life. Princeton's Graduate School was formally established in 1901, but as long ago as colonial times, an occasional student would remain after graduation to prepare for the ministry with the college president. Construction of the residence halls began in May 1911. This stately collection of Gothic buildings includes the 173-foot Cleveland Tower, erected as a memorial to President Grover Cleveland, a trustee of the university. The tower's beauty has been compared to that of Oxford's Magdalen Tower.

Each Sunday afternoon, chapel music from the tower's sixty-seven cast bronze carillon bells, installed in 1927 as a gift from the Class of 1892, can be heard throughout town. During winter, the slopes of the adjacent golf course are filled with children sledding down snow-covered hills. Warmer months find golfers hitting the links just a few blocks from the center of town—all within the shadow of the magnificent tower on the hill, from which can still be seen Beatrix Farrand's pleasing natural vistas.

the tower

Now that the three- or four-hundred year old Mercer oak

has suddenly done a disappearing act

and given way under its black cloak

as a magician might suddenly succumb to his own magic, a tactician to his tact,

I cast about for an image of the present age

that might sustain

comparison with some ancient site of pilgrimage,

Stonehenge or Salisbury, only to catch it in the squared-off stain

on the retina, impossible to raze,

of the tower of the Graduate College.

EXCERPT FROM *THE TOWER* MAY 2000
— PAUL MULDOON (1951-)
IN CELEBRATION OF THE GRADUATE COLLEGE'S CENTENNIAL (2001–2002)

in the pink

When my neighbor Nora Orphanides, a former director of the board of the University Medical Center at Princeton's Foundation, told me about the proposed Breast Health Center, I contacted Betsy Sands, president of the Women's Auxiliary, and offered to plan their first fund-raiser. The medical center is a local resource that we often take for granted—especially the services of the emergency room. When you're a new mother, there's a sense of security in knowing that a doctor is just five minutes away. One of my most memorable visits was for an X-ray of five-year-old Christopher's abdomen, in search of his lost marble. Its location remains an unsolved mystery.

As we considered locations for this fund-raiser, Liz Hosny's September garden seemed the perfect space. We approached her to host the luncheon, and she agreed to once again open her garden gate to the community. Susan designed a birdhouse-inspired invitation wrapped in gentle words by Kozuko Okakura. The bright blue and green invitations were tied with a contrasting pink ribbon symbolizing breast cancer awareness. Two hundred invitations were mailed with the U.S. Postal Service's "Fund the Cure" stamp, designed by Ethel Kessler of Bethesda, Maryland. Our friend David Porat, owner of Chelsea Market Baskets in New York City, donated exquisitely decorated gift boxes filled with English jams, teas, and biscuits as a party favor for each guest. Prizes were solicited for a small silent auction: Shelley Roe and Sam Miller donated colorful birdhouses, and local nurseries offered gardening gifts.

IN THE PINK FOR BREAST CANCER AWARENESS
During the 1500s, pink symbolized
the embodiment of perfection.
Today the expression signifies good health.

At the luncheon, guest speaker Dr. Rachel Dultz, head of the planned facility, spoke to guests about her commitment to offering local treatments. According to Dr. Dultz, "This new facility will provide all aspects of care, including diagnosis, clinical treatment, psychosocial support and education."

One hundred percent of the donations were passed along to the hospital auxiliary in support of the breast health center. As tables shaded by the large market umbrellas filled with friends and neighbors sharing our Provençal-inspired buffet, the sunshine and clear skies of the last days of summer warmed Liz's garden, and it once again became a center of hope.

luncheon in the garden

Liz and Zaki own a second home in Provence, so they have an obvious fondness for the Provençal style of entertaining. To me, this meant a comfortable casual environment, lunch in the garden on a glorious sun-filled day, and a menu planned with the freshest ingredients. The luncheon was served buffet-style on a long table set under the wisteria-covered arbor beside the pool. Attached to the new garage, the vine-covered natural awning created a shaded area for pool guests and was the perfect spot for outdoor entertaining. The narrow pool resembles a reflection pool and is surrounded by tall antique olive *jarres* imported from Provence by Liz's friend Leslie Wehr of Thyme on the Terrace, located in the scenic Brandywine Valley in West Chester, Pennsylvania.

Rather than blocking the view of the garden, we filled the pebble driveway with small round tables gathered to resemble a café setting. Market umbrellas were scattered about for shade, and Liz selected a soft combination of tablecloths in an earthy green with a sheer cream patterned topper. Mary Harrison of Euphorbia, a party and event planning business in Lawrenceville, found luncheon and dessert plates designed with small watering cans and garden trowels floating on the rim. To tie in the touch of pink associated with breast cancer awareness, guests were offered a welcoming glass of pink champagne at the garden entrance. Afterward, a refreshing mango iced tea was served.

(ABOVE AND RIGHT) Liz's bright blue birdhouse tree inspired the graphics. The invitation, Breast Health Center information, and reply card were tucked neatly into a birdhouse-shaped pouch. Buffet food was identifed using a similar design. A pink ribbon served as a visual reminder of the benefit.

This menu represents my general philosophy of large-scale entertaining: Variety is the key to a successful buffet. Don't be afraid to offer a wide selection of food choices. Guests will usually surprise you and enjoy trying a taste of everything. When selecting the menu for a buffet, relax and experiment a little. If one dish isn't a big hit, chances are the next recipe will be. Along with a few traditional and expected salads, we tossed in a few new ideas, all based on the Provençal style of cooking that has made the area so famous—the freshest ingredients combined in a classic but simple way. This style of cooking uses no butter, no cream, no flour, no heavy sauces, a few potatoes, a few eggs, a little red meat, lots of fresh fruit and vegetables, fresh seafood, freshly picked herbs, a few spices, and light reductions of wine and stock. Of course, everything is cooked, dressed, marinated, and bathed in a sublime French olive oil, then served in earthenware dishes.

(PREVIOUS PAGE LEFT) Shaded by the wisteria-covered trellis, the Provençal-inspired buffet table.

(PREVIOUS PAGE RIGHT) An earthenware dish from Liz's collection, filled with Roasted Corn, Tomato, and Cucumber Salad.

(LEFT) Chicken Salad with Red Grapes and Walnuts on a croissant from the Witherspoon Bread Company.

(RIGHT TOP) Ratatouille Frittata.

(RIGHT CENTER) Mediterranean Angel-Hair Pasta with Mussels.

(RIGHT BOTTOM) Grilled Tuna Niçoise Salad.

Cobb salad. A combination of summer-sweet Silver Queen corn, fresh tomatoes, and crunchy cucumbers brought us back home. Standing tall above the buffet was Liz's antique olive *jarre*, overflowing with an arrangement of giant sunflowers designed by Liz's friend Meg Wislar, owner of Boxwood Gardens.

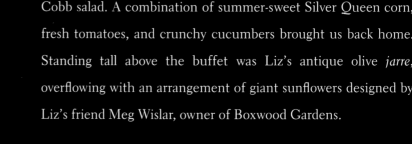

(LEFT TOP) We chose one of Liz's favorite hand-painted earthenware dishes for the Citrusy Couscous Salad.

(LEFT CENTER) Focaccia filled with fresh grilled vegetables, tomatoes, and mozzarella cheese.

(LEFT BOTTOM) Basque Bean and Sausage Salad.

(LEFT) Betsy Wislar of Boxwood Gardens filled Liz's tall antique *jarre* with the colors of Provence.

(RIGHT TOP) Liz's neighbor Anne Reeves chats with Jean Huntington and another party guest.

(RIGHT BOTTOM) French doors were added to the living room to welcome the garden view.

(FOLLOWING PAGE LEFT) A hand-painted sugar cookie, inspired by Liz's birdhouse tree collection.

(FOLLOWING PAGE RIGHT) Annie B's Bee Skep Lemon-Meringue Tartlets.

annie b's surprise ending

Since we are often tempted to eat dessert first, it is fitting that Annie B should have the final say with a special recipe. In the spring of 2004, Ann had told me enthusiastically about a new dessert she was preparing. She suggested I come to her Newtown, Pennsylvania, bakery and take a look at her creations. Intrigued, I drove to her professional-sized bakery. Inside her walk-in, room-sized freezer sat five hundred small baked Alaskas, shaped like beehives, twirled with golden meringue tops and tiny handmade marzipan bees perched on top. I happily walked away with several to photograph in my garden and eventually enjoy.

When Liz decided to host the fund-raiser in her garden, I called Annie B, and she agreed to make this clever dessert in miniature form for our September garden party—but she added a surprise twist. Instead of filling them with the traditional ice cream, in honor of our Provençal theme, she used creamy lemon curd. These delicate tartlets were the prize treat of our dessert table, along with her painted birdhouse-shaped sugar cookies and crunchy lemon-almond biscotti coated with a

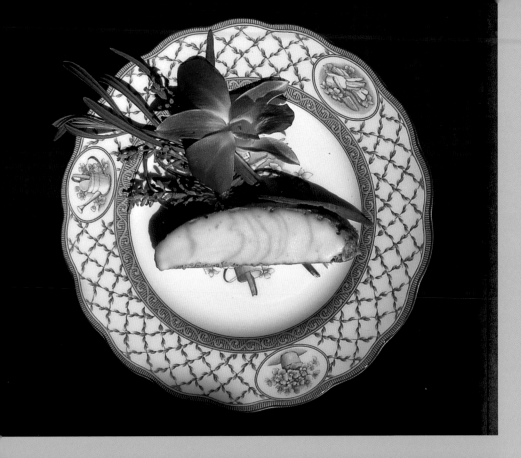

delicate lavender glaze. Through her creative use of regional ingredients such as lemon, almond, and lavender, Annie B brought in so many elements of the South of France that we now call her our Queen Bee. The presentation of more than two hundred baby beehives brought happy oohs and aahs from our astonished guests as they savored their last bit of Provence before leaving Eden to return to the real world and the quiet tree-lined streets of Princeton. When they accepted their gift box, a token of our appreciation, and exited the garden through the vine-covered gate, it was apparent that Liz and her friends and neighbors understood the meaning of the inscription that graces the gates to Beatrix Farrand's premier garden, Dumbarton Oaks: *Quod Severis Metes*—As you sow, so shall you reap.

(LEFT TOP) Lemon-Almond Biscotti with
a sheer lavender glaze.

(LEFT BOTTOM) Each guest received an exquisite
box filled with English jams, teas, and biscuits.

(RIGHT) The 1915 stucco house is painted a soft cream
with green shutters, reminiscent of the olive trees in Provence.

(FOLLOWING PAGE LEFT) The garden sculpture
representing Liz and Zaki's son, Mark.

There is no "The End" to be written, neither can you,

like an architect, engrave in stone the day the garden

was finished; a painter can frame his picture, a composer

notate his coda, but a garden is always on the move.

–Mirabel Osler

The most wonderful thing I will remember about Drumthwacket, now the New Jersey Governor's Mansion, is that it was once home to a beautiful golden-haired child named Agnes Taylor Pyne. Her father, Moses Taylor Pyne, Jr., and his brothers, Percy Rivington and Robert Stockton, were children in this grand house and played in its formal Italianate gardens, with numerous ponds

and wooded hills. When Agie, as her friends knew her, visited her grandfather's country estate for the last time, she was almost eighty years old and living in Flower Mound, Texas. She shared stories of her childhood and memories of life at her grandfather's country estate in Princeton with Daphne Townsend, former executive director of the Drumthwacket Foundation.

For Agnes, Drumthwacket, with its massive but comfortable house, abundant woods, and gardens, was a magical place. There were endless hidden spaces to explore, goldfish ponds to swim in, frogs to catch, and a marble pergola for afternoon doll tea parties. Her grandfather's prestige and inherited wealth provided Agnes with a childhood and adult life of unimaginable privilege and social dominance during the Gilded Age of America (1865–1929) and what is often referred to as Princeton's Golden Age (1890–1930).

The only grandchild of Moses Taylor Pyne and Margaretta Stockton Pyne, and the only child of Moses Taylor Pyne, Jr., and Agnes Griswold Landon Pyne, Agnes married Princeton graduate Robert O. Bacon at Princeton's Trinity Episcopal Church on June 9, 1934, in a ceremony attended by New York, Philadelphia, and Newport society. Her wedding breakfast and reception were held at Drumthwacket, where her widowed grandmother lived. The *New York Herald-Tribune* reported that the wedding united "two illustrious families." Since both Agnes's father and grandfather were deceased, her uncle Percy R. Pyne II gave her away. A

(PRECEDING PAGE) A view of the Solarium from the rear gardens of Drumthwacket.

(LEFT) Captured in a pensive moment, Agnes Taylor Pyne stands beside one of the numerous ponds and lakes that were once part of the Drumthwacket estate.
PHOTO COURTESY OF COLLECTIONS OF THE DRUMTHWACKET FOUNDATION.

(ABOVE) Miniature on ivory of Moses Taylor Pyne.
PHOTO COURTESY OF COLLECTIONS OF THE DRUMTHWACKET FOUNDATION.

(FOLLOWING PAGE LEFT) Princeton University Class of 1877 reunion.
COLLECTIONS OF THE DRUMTHWACKET FOUNDATION.

photograph of the large wedding party, which included twelve bridesmaids, is still displayed in the library of the Governor's Mansion. Unfortunately, this would not be the only marriage for Agnes. In the end, her heart belonged to Texan Lawrence Davis. In one of her last visits with Daphne, Agnes bragged about her homemade pickles winning first prize at the Texas State Fair in Dallas. She gave Daphne a tour of the town of Flower Mound, and of Green Acres, the farm she shared with Larry—thousands of miles and a lifetime away from the eastern society life she had

The New Jersey Governor's Mansion, Drumthwacket (Scots Gaelic for "wooded hills"), was built on land once owned by William Penn. It was purchased in 1696 by local resident William Olden, a member of one of the six Quaker families who settled at Stony Brook around 1685. Olden's grandson Thomas purchased a portion of the land that included the small homestead that now serves as the Drumthwacket Foundation headquarters. The property would eventually pass to Thomas's grandson Charles Smith Olden, who is believed to have been born there in 1799.

area of Princeton, Charles and his wife, Phoebe Ann Smith, built their impressive estate, Drumthwacket, and called it home for the remainder of their lives. Charles built the center portion of what is now Drumthwacket in 1835, modeling it after Greek Revival homes he had seen in the New Orleans Garden District, with a large portico and six detailed ionic columns. An active business, community, and political leader, he was also the treasurer and trustee of Princeton University, a state senator, and then governor of New Jersey in 1860. Charles was a close friend of President Abraham Lincoln and a strong opponent of slavery. He died in 1876. His widow sold the estate to prominent industrialist and banker Moses Taylor Pyne in 1893.

Pyne's immense wealth came from his maternal grandfather, Moses Taylor, who was the first president of the National City Bank of New York and the principal stockholder in the Delaware, Lackawanna, and Western Railroad Company. He was said to have been worth over $40 million when he died in 1882. Pyne was one of the first business commuters to New York City, traveling in grand style on his personal train, the *Pyne Express*, which he kept next

(ABOVE) Bookplate of Moses Taylor Pyne: the library at Drumthwacket. COURTESY OF PRINCETON UNIVERSITY LIBRARY.

to Blair Arch on the Princeton University campus. His love of Princeton University (Class of 1877) inspired him to move from New York and transform Drumthwacket into one of the premier private properties in Princeton. He added two wings, elaborate gardens, and six major outbuildings. The three-hundred-acre estate was maintained by thirty gardeners and became a model farm, with extensive landscaping, under the guidance of architect Raleigh C. Gildersleeve. The outbuildings included a coach house and stables, a greenhouse and potting shed, a garden building, the gardener's house, a farmer's house and dairy, and a cow barn. Pyne added hundreds of acres, which included parklike landscaping, bridle paths, and formal Italianate gardens. The Pynes' family life was grandiose and extravagant beyond anything Princeton's more traditional society had ever experienced.

remnants of the past

Today, as you drive down Mercer Road between Lover's Lane and Stony Brook Road, you will pass numerous Tudor-style buildings that have merged into comfortable but unique family residences. Architect Glen Fries and his wife, Ann,

live with their two children in the restored farmer's house and dairy on Parkside Drive. Ralph Lerner, a professor of architectural design at Princeton University's School of Architecture and its dean from 1989 to 2002, lives with his architect wife, Lisa Fischetti, and their two children behind the dairy in the restored and strikingly contemporary cow barn. One of the garden buildings with a distinctive brick turret and copper accents still stands next to the Tudor-style gardener's cottage. The potting shed, the only remaining portion of the once massive greenhouse structure, now sits alone as a quaint cottage. These three buildings are located, appropriately, on Greenhouse Road and are all maintained as private residences.

Around the corner on Lover's Lane, near what was once the main gate, is the recently restored coach house. You can still see remnants of the rhododendron-lined path that led to the informal side gate used by local visitors. These surviving outbuildings are preserved as family homes, in a part of Princeton and Drumthwacket's intertwined history.

(LEFT TOP) The "happy picture," circa 1920:
Moses Taylor Pyne, Jr. (1885–1923);
Moses Taylor Pyne, Sr. (1855–1921);
Agnes Taylor Pyne Davis (1915–1994);
Agnes Griswold Landon Pyne (1887–1961);
Margaretta Stockton Pyne (1856–1939);
and an unidentified uncle.
COLLECTIONS OF THE DRUMTHWACKET FOUNDATION.

(LEFT BOTTOM) Called the Temple of Love,
the white marble pergola on the Upper
Pond was the perfect spot for a tea party.
COLLECTIONS OF THE DRUMTHWACKET FOUNDATION.

(RIGHT) Written on the back of the
photograph: "It was fun swimming
with the goldfish, signed Agnes."
COLLECTIONS OF THE DRUMTHWACKET FOUNDATION.

(FOLLOWING PAGE LEFT) Map of the
Drumthwacket estate, 1905. COLLECTIONS OF
THE HISTORICAL SOCIETY OF PRINCETON.

(FOLLOWING PAGE RIGHT) The Pyne boys
(left to right): Percy Rivington Pyne II; Moses
Taylor Pyne, Jr.; and Robert Stockton Pyne.
COLLECTIONS OF THE DRUMTHWACKET FOUNDATION.

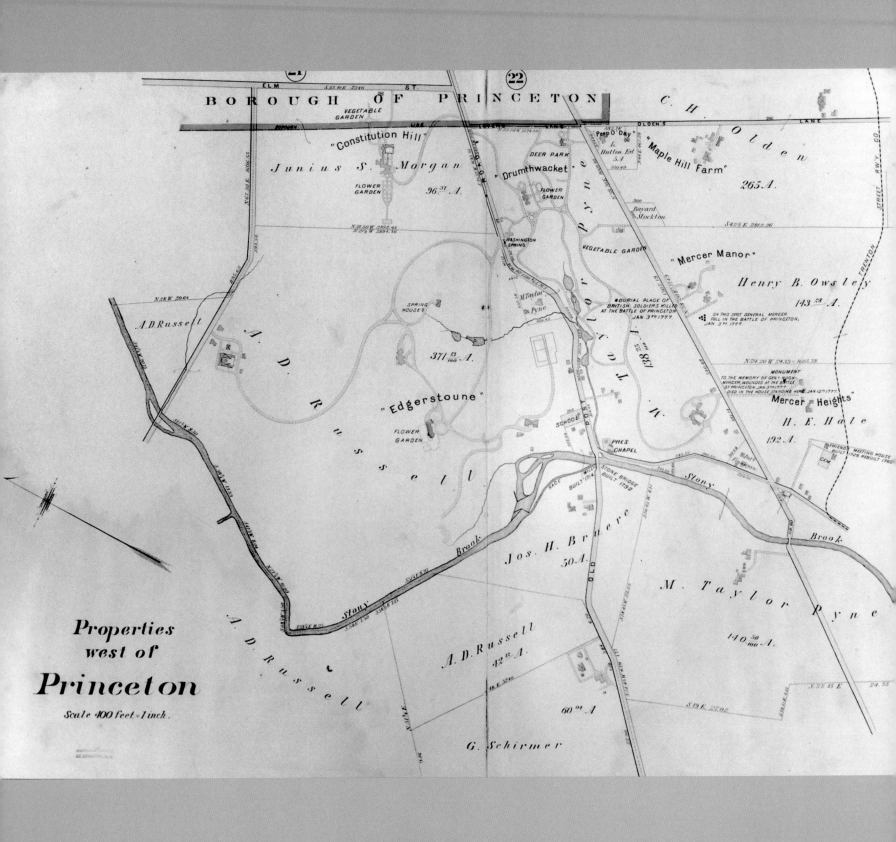

Properties west of Princeton

Scale 400 feet = 1 inch.

BOROUGH OF PRINCETON

"Constitution Hill"

Junius S. Morgan

96 A.

"Drumthwacket"

DEER PARK

"Peep O'Day"

"Maple Hill Farm"

265 A.

"Mercer Manor"

Henry B. Owsley

143 A.

A. D. Russell

SPRING HOUSE

371 A.

"Edgerstoune"

FLOWER GARDEN

VEGETABLE GARDEN

BURIAL PLACE OF BRITISH SOLDIERS KILLED AT THE BATTLE OF PRINCETON JAN 3RD 1777

ON THIS SPOT GENERAL MERCER FELL IN THE BATTLE OF PRINCETON, JAN 3RD 1777

138 A.

Mercer Heights

H. E. Hale

192 A.

SCHOOL

PRES. CHAPEL

MILLSTONE BRIDGE BUILT 1792

Stony

Brook

Jos. H. Bruere

50 A.

A. D. Russell

42 A.

60 A.

G. Schirmer

M. Taylor Pyne

140 A.

On Sunday afternoons, the Pynes opened their estate grounds (except for the formal upper terrace) to town families. The gardens were planted to bloom continually from May through September. Visitors strolled the winding path from Lover's Lane, enjoying the herd of deer maintained in the deer park and the caged black and white squirrels, which always somehow managed to escape. Farther into the grounds, there was a series of ponds surrounded by flowering trees and plants reflecting in the water. Each pond was filled with hundreds of lotus flowers, floating swans, and ducks. The paths wound up at the dairy farm by the Stony Brook, where grassy meadows were covered with grazing sheep and prizewinning cows.

I can only imagine the local children's excitement as they approached the aviary of rare birds and the monkey house. Knowing the mischief that little kids can get into, they probably also chased the peacocks and swans that drifted freely on the expansive front and back lawns. Princeton resident Albert Hines, who turned 102 this year, says that visiting the gardens of Drumthwacket was "just about the only thing there was to do in Princeton on a Sunday afternoon back then." He remembers walking through the estate grounds and then taking the Nassau Street trolley to the city of Trenton. It seems that for all of Princeton, the grounds

were used as a town park and public gathering space. Continuing this tradition, a portion of the estate would become part of Princeton's Battlefield State Park on Mercer Road.

As Dale and I searched through the Drumthwacket Foundation's archives, Lisa Paine, the newly appointed director, shared a photograph of Agnes taken near the upper pond around 1920. It captured the elegance of life at Drumthwacket: the beautiful child in her crisp, starched Sunday dress prepared by a servant, her hair perfectly curled and ribboned by a loving nanny, gazing for the photographer at the lotus-filled garden pond that was maintained by a staff of thirty gardeners. This portrait became the focal point for our story about the influential Pyne family and their country home. Prior to her death in 1994, just shy of her eightieth birthday, Agnes donated a personal collection of family photographs to the foundation. As I searched through these images, I came across a handwritten note that said simply, "I enjoyed growing up at Drumthwacket, signed Agnes."

And to judge from the tales that she told Daphne on her last visit to the estate, enjoy it she did: morning rides on the bridle paths, skating on the frozen ponds in winter, summer tennis and

(LEFT, RIGHT TOP, RIGHT BOTTOM) Eastern stair at grotto; fountain looking south; balustrade elements south wall. The garden restoration project was begun by Lucinda Florio and completed under the guidance of landscape architect Paul Dorko of Hidden Valley Nurseries in Stockton, New Jersey. COURTESY OF LIBRARY OF CONGRESS. DAN CORNISH, PHOTOGRAPHER.

The
DRUMTHWACKET
F O U N D A T I O N

established 1982

PLEASE RESPOND BEFORE MAY 30

accepts   M   regrets

resting place

swimming with her best friend, Sally—who lived at the Morgan estate across the street—capturing frogs and chasing peacocks throughout the gardens. But for Agnes, this place wasn't just a lavish country estate—it was her grandparents' home.

best-loved alum

Moses Taylor Pyne was considered Princeton University's best-known and best-loved Princeton alumnus. Pyne devoted most of his adult life and much of his personal fortune to establishing Princeton as a major university: Between 1890 and 1920, Pyne emerged as its most powerful administrator. Agnes lost her grandfather on April 22, 1921. The day of his funeral, all university activities were suspended, and business stopped on Nassau Street. Town church bells rang all day long. The funeral procession passed through a student guard of honor that led to the hallowed Nassau Hall. The Pyne Honor Prize was founded in 1921 in his honor and is still the university's most prestigious award, given annually to a senior who best demonstrates "scholastic excellence, strength of character and support for the interests of the University."

Agnes called the circa-1920 family portrait taken on the front steps of Drumthwacket her "happy picture." Her grandfather died in 1921 and her father died in 1923, just after his thirty-eighth birthday; even the beloved family dog died shortly after

the photograph was taken. Agnes's grandmother Margaretta continued to live and entertain at the estate, but in a more modest manner. Locals called her the White Queen, a reference to her customary dress color and her charming but eccentric demeanor, said to be similar to the "fuzzy-mindedness" of Lewis Carroll's character. The family's devoted butler, Englishman Henry Egglesfield, continued to run the house and serve dinner guests at Mrs. Pyne's parties, despite developing palsy. Guests apparently learned to cover themselves well with napkins to avoid the more than occasional spills. But the expense of operating an extensive staff was considerable, and after the Depression, even the richest Americans found their expensive lifestyles difficult to maintain. New estate and income taxes initiated by Woodrow Wilson's administration were depleting many family fortunes.

(PRECEDING PAGE LEFT) Susan designed the gatefold invitation with Agnes's love of discovery in mind—each layer unfolding until the magical image of Agnes in her garden is revealed. A crisp, cotton bow peeked out of the top, reminiscent of Agnes's hair ribbons.

(LEFT) Agnes Taylor Pyne with her mother, Agnes Griswold Landon Pyne, in the marble Temple of Love, which was built on the Upper Pond and was part of the original estate gardens. It has been restored and is part of a neighboring property.
COURTESY OF COLLECTION OF THE DRUMTHWACKET FOUNDATION.

(RIGHT) The menu featured an image of Agnes's fountain and brought the white, butterfly-like bows to the table.

Menu

CREAMY TOMATO *and* CARROT SOUP
JACK'S LOBSTER SALAD
TEXAS CHOCOLATE CAKE
MUM'S SIPPIN' WHISKEY

(PRECEDING PAGE LEFT) A dining table in the Solarium set to merge old and new ideas about entertaining: 1941 Moonstone goblets and late-nineteenth-century sterling flatware alongside contemporary linens, pottery plates, and etched star glasses.

(LEFT TOP) Filled with roses, floral swags, columns, and flutes, Towle's 1898 Georgian sterling flatware pattern is reminiscent of the prosperity during the reign of King George V of Great Britain (1865–1936).

(LEFT BOTTOM) Champagne grapes, endive spears, and an edible flower decorate a luxurious lobster salad.

(RIGHT) Creamy Carrot and Tomato Soup garnished with fresh herbs from the Drumthwacket herb garden.

Wednesday-afternoon tours continue, and busloads of excited schoolchildren arrive to see the house that Charles Smith Olden built in 1835.

The world is filled with constant reminders of generations past, and it is our responsibility to pay close attention to these sometimes forgotten spaces. We must recognize that they, too, were once filled with important moments in the lives of those who also passed this way and were once part of our community. Moses Taylor Pyne's spirit of community, along with his apparent appreciation of the natural beauty of Princeton, thrive in the restored house and garden. This space now belongs to the people of New Jersey, and the renovated gardens are once again filled with appreciative neighbors. It is fitting that the Frog Pond, a secluded space located at the bottom of the manicured terrace, with a panoramic view of the upper gardens, is dedicated to Agnes. There is a sense of tranquility and peace in this serene spot, and if you sit there quietly on a summer afternoon, you might perceive a soft but mischievous giggle as the memory of Moses Taylor Pyne's beautiful grandchild drifts throughout this still-enchanted space.

(RIGHT) A second view of the Solarium with a statue of Narcissus donated to Drumthwacket by Agnes Taylor Pyne Davis.

(FOLLOWING PAGE LEFT) The statue of a little boy fishing is original to the Frog Pond and also was donated by Agnes Taylor Pyne Davis.

more than
a country residence

I learned a great deal about New Jersey's history and local architecture throughout my stint as a docent during Governor Christie Todd Whitman's administration. I was responsible for the Music Room for holiday tours (as the junior docent in the house, I was given that room because it was small, sparsely furnished, and an easy room to memorize). Before and after tours, I often had a chance to enjoy the view from the Solarium at the rear of the formal main hallway. If I were a resident of this grand house, that is where I would spend my free time: A morning cup of coffee or an evening glass of wine, while gazing out onto the restored historical garden, would be a perfect way to begin or end any day. I wondered if the governor and her husband ever used the space for a private breakfast or dinner. The room was once the outdoor dining room, which the Pynes temporarily enclosed during the winter months, but to me, it was a space full of entertaining possibilities.

Originally, we planned a luncheon for the members of the New Jersey garden clubs who volunteer to decorate the house for special holiday tours throughout the year. We were working with Lisa Paine, executive director of the foundation, on a casually elegant gathering to be held in the Solarium. Unfortunately, security in the house became an issue after

September 11, 2001, and while we were able to photograph the table settings and food, the luncheon was indefinitely postponed. A new governor was elected that fall, and since he and his family opted to reside in the mansion, our access to the house was limited. But because of Drumthwacket and the Pyne family's historical significance to Princeton and the state of New Jersey, we wanted to share the story of this space.

The reality is that none of us could have lunch in the Solarium at Drumthwacket, unless, of course, we were friends or family of the residing governor. But the house is a public domain, owned by the state, and a space to be enjoyed by all residents of New Jersey. Weekly and holiday tours have resumed, and visitors can once again experience the architectural beauty, learn about the Revolutionary War and New Jersey's history, and stroll through the gardens. They can shop for souvenirs in the landmark Olden House and imagine what the space was like when it was an aviary of rare birds and a monkey house. They can ponder how loyal butler Henry Egglesfield and his family of ten children managed, even for a short period of time, to live in such a small house. Children are once again exploring hidden places and enjoying the Frog Pond. And for the fourth time in its extended history, Drumthwacket is a gathering place that is home to a prominent family but enjoyed by all.

The house [Drumthwacket]

itself is delightful

and is more than a mere country

residence; it is a home,

with all the charm

that the word connotates,

possessing a gracious presence

which seems to bespeak a welcome

for the frequent guests who pass its

hospitable threshold.

— FRANCES BENJAMIN JOHNSON, *TOWN & COUNTRY*, CA. 1910

(PRECEDING PAGE) The Frog Pond was dedicated to
Agnes Taylor Pyne Davis on July 15, 1997.

(LEFT) Visitors to the mansion are greeted by an
exquisitely carved Greek Revival front door, circa 1835.

(RIGHT) Statues representing the four seasons are placed
throughout the garden's stone paths.

recipeas *for you*

My kitchen is a mystical place, a kind of temple for me.
It is a place where the surfaces seem to have significance,
where the sounds and odors carry meaning
that transfers from the past and bridges to the future.

— PEARL BAILEY (1918–1990)

Crab and Capellini Balls with Jalapeño-Lime Sauce

These crunchy little balls are an economical and distinctive way to include crab at your next party. Be sure to chill the balls well, so they hold together when frying. Serve with Jalapeño-Lime dipping sauce.

½ pound capellini or vermicelli pasta

1 pound fresh cooked lump crabmeat, drained

3 green onions, trimmed and finely chopped

4 large eggs, lightly beaten

¾ cup freshly grated Parmesan cheese, loosely packed

1 teaspoon salt, plus more for seasoning

½ teaspoon pepper, freshly ground

Cayenne pepper to taste

2 quarts safflower oil for deep-frying

Jalapeño-Lime Sauce (RECIPEA FOLLOWS)

Cook the pasta according to package directions until al dente. Drain, rinse with cold water, and set aside.

In a bowl, mix together the next seven ingredients, then add the pasta. Toss with your hands, breaking up the pasta slightly and making sure the ingredients are well mixed. Form into Ping-Pong-sized balls and place on a parchment- or foil-lined baking sheet. Refrigerate for a few hours until very firm, or freeze for about 30 minutes.

When ready to serve, heat oil in a 3-quart saucepan or deep fryer to 350°F. Cook a few crab balls at a time until golden, about 1 minute. (Note: If the balls don't hold together when frying, stop and chill them again

until completely firm.) Carefully remove from the pan with a slotted spoon and drain on paper towels. Sprinkle immediately with salt, if desired. After removing each batch, allow the oil to return to 350°F. Keep warm in a 150°F oven until all the crab balls are cooked. Serve warm with Jalapeño-Lime Sauce.

Pasta mixture can be made a day ahead and refrigerated, covered tightly with plastic wrap. Crab balls can also be cooked ahead and reheated in a 400°F oven for 4–5 minutes or until warm.

MAKES 4 DOZEN

JALAPEÑO-LIME SAUCE

½ cup fresh lime juice

6 tablespoons fermented fish sauce (*nam pla*)*

¼ cup maple syrup or honey

3 fresh jalapeño peppers, seeded and finely chopped

2 garlic cloves, finely chopped

Mix all ingredients in large bowl to blend. Cover and chill at least 1 hour or overnight to develop flavors.

Nam pla can be found in specialty stores or the Asian section of many large supermarkets. You may also substitute the more readily available Thai fish sauce.

MAKES ABOUT 1 CUP

Grilled Baby Lamb Chops with Fresh Tomato-Mint Relish

There is something tantalizing about being served a tiny lamp chop at a cocktail party. This is a luxury hors d'oeuvre, to be reserved for very special occasions. Marinated in olive oil, garlic, and rosemary, these bite-size grilled chops are divine. The Tomato-Mint Relish adds a traditional touch of mint.

½ cup olive oil, plus 2 tablespoons

3 large garlic cloves, minced

2 tablespoons fresh rosemary, finely chopped

24 baby lamb chops, trimmed and with bones Frenched

Vegetable oil spray

Salt and freshly ground pepper to taste

Fresh Tomato-Mint Relish (RECIPEA FOLLOWS)

Whisk together ½ cup olive oil, garlic, and rosemary and pour over chops. Refrigerate, covered, for at least 4 hours or preferably overnight, turning once. Drain chops and return to room temperature before grilling.

When ready to cook, heat the outdoor grill or indoor grill pan to medium (if you're cooking indoors, do the chops in batches, taking care not to crowd the pan). Coat the grates with vegetable spray to prevent sticking. Brush the chops lightly with the remaining 2 tablespoons of olive oil, and season with salt and pepper on both sides. Cook 3–5 minutes per side, turning once with tongs. The chops should register 120°F to 135°F at the thickest part for rare to medium-rare. Remove from grill and let rest for 5 minutes before serving.

To prepare ahead, cook to 120°F for rare, and refrigerate tightly covered. When ready to serve, reheat in a 400°F oven for 5–6 minutes, depending on thickness. Top with Fresh Tomato-Mint Relish and serve warm.

SERVES 12 AS AN HORS D'OEUVRE

FRESH TOMATO-MINT RELISH

4 Roma tomatoes, seeded and diced

1 tablespoon garlic, minced

1 tablespoon balsamic vinegar

¼ cup olive oil

Salt and freshly ground pepper to taste

1 tablespoon fresh mint, finely chopped

Mix all ingredients in a nonreactive bowl and set aside for flavors to blend, about 30 minutes.

MAKES APPROXIMATELY 1 CUP

Fig and Gorgonzola Phyllo Triangles

Many cooks are afraid of working with phyllo, but these paper-thin sheets of dough are very forgiving and provide a flaky golden hors d'oeuvre that just can't be duplicated. The combination of figs, sweet onions, and Gorgonzola cheese is unforgettable.

1 cup dried mission or calimyrna figs, diced

½ cup golden raisins

½ cup apricot nectar

⅓ cup honey

2 tablespoons unsalted butter, cold

2 cups sweet onions (from 1 large onion), coarsely chopped

2 tablespoons balsamic vinegar

½ cup (4 ounces) crumbled blue cheese, such as Gorgonzola

1 16-ounce package frozen phyllo dough,
    thawed in refrigerator according to package instructions

2 sticks unsalted butter, melted

Preheat oven to 350°F. Line two baking sheets with parchment paper and set aside.

Bring figs, raisins, apricot nectar, and honey to a boil. Remove from heat, transfer to a large bowl, and let stand for 30 minutes until cool.

Heat 2 tablespoons of the cold butter in a medium sauté pan over medium heat, then add the onion. Cook, stirring occasionally, until the onion begins to brown, about 15 minutes. Add the balsamic vinegar and continue to sauté until deep golden brown, approximately 20–25 minutes

total, stirring frequently. Remove from heat, transfer to a large bowl, and cool completely. Stir in the cooled fig mixture and crumbled blue cheese. Set aside.

Gently unroll the thawed phyllo dough, cover with a piece of waxed paper, then top with a damp dishcloth. Remove one phyllo sheet and place on your work surface with the long side closest to you, taking care to completely cover the unused phyllo. Using a pastry brush, lightly brush the entire sheet with melted butter. Add a second sheet of phyllo and butter, then repeat with a third layer.

Cut the dough vertically into 6 short rectangles. Place a scant tablespoon of fig mixture on the bottom right edge of the phyllo strips. Fold the bottom right corner over the filling to meet the left side, as you would fold a flag, forming a triangle. Continue folding triangles until you reach the edge, sealing the end of the sheet with melted butter. Place two inches apart on the parchment-paper-lined baking sheet and continue until all the fig mixture is used. Cover prepared triangles with plastic wrap or a clean dish towel while working.

Phyllo triangles can be prepared to this point and frozen. If freezing, separate each layer with a sheet of waxed or parchment paper.

When ready to serve, brush the freshly made or frozen triangles with melted butter and bake 15–20 minutes or until golden. Serve warm. Phyllo triangles can be cooked a few hours ahead and reheated in a 350°F oven for 5–6 minutes, or until warm.

MAKES ABOUT 4 DOZEN

CHAPTER TWO *birds of a feather*

A "Dressed" Baked Brie

Chilling the Brie in the refrigerator overnight makes slicing it easier and much safer. Use any leftover puff pastry to decorate the top. Cookie cutters are a great decorating tool for seasonal themes. We added a cutout dress to our Baked Brie to emphasize one of Sunny's Ruby Pearl designs. Brushed with a beaten egg white, the puff pastry bakes to a shiny golden brown. This is an excellent hors d'oeuvre for large parties and can be made ahead of time.

1 sheet frozen puff pastry (half of a 17.3-ounce package),
    thawed according to package instructions
1 32-ounce Brie wheel, well chilled
¾ cup chutney*
1 large egg white
Baguette slices or crackers

To prevent sticking, lightly dust the work surface and rolling pin with 1 to 2 tablespoons of flour. Place one sheet of puff pastry on the work surface. Using the floured rolling pin, roll the pastry into a ⅛-inch-thick square, approximately 14 inches in each direction.

Remove the chilled cheese from all packaging and paper. Using a long serrated knife, slowly and carefully slice the Brie round horizontally in half, ending up with two complete rounds. Spoon the chutney on the middle of one round, spreading to within ½ inch of the outside edges.

Place the second round on top, wiping off any filling that oozes out the sides. Center the stuffed Brie on the rolled-out puff pastry square and gently pull the pastry sides up and into the center, pinching the edges together to seal. The Brie should be entirely covered in puff pastry. Slice off and reserve any excess pastry. Carefully turn the Brie over and place on a baking sheet. Cut out decorative patterns with any remaining puff pastry and place on top. Cover lightly with plastic wrap and refrigerate for at least 30 minutes. It can be made one day ahead to this point, covered well with plastic wrap, and refrigerated overnight.

When ready to cook, preheat oven to 400°F. Lightly beat the egg white. Using a pastry brush, brush the top and sides of the puff pastry with egg. Bake for 20–25 minutes, or until puff pastry is a light golden brown and the cheese is warmed but not oozing. Remove from the oven and let sit for at least 15 minutes before serving. Brie can be made ahead and served at room temperature. Serve with baguette slices or crackers.

*Use your favorite spicy fruit chutney or jam. We used half each of the Bay Tree Food Company's caramelized peppers and caramelized onions, available from Chelsea Market Baskets (see *Resources*).

SERVES 12 AS AN HORS D'OEUVRE

Jack's Miniature Crab Cakes with Roasted Garlic Aioli

Since this was a last-minute party for more than fifty, I decided to purchase miniature crab cakes from Nassau Street Seafood. Owner Jack Morrison is the premier supplier of fresh seafood in the Princeton area, traveling several times a week to the New York or Philadelphia fish markets. He generously shared his recipe for this popular hors d'oeuvre. Old Bay seasoning, a blend of spices developed over sixty years ago in the Chesapeake Bay area, specifically for crab lovers, gives these little cakes the perfect lift.

2 large eggs

1 cup mayonnaise

1 tablespoon Dijon mustard

1 cup Japanese bread crumbs*

2 pounds lump crabmeat

1 teaspoon Old Bay seasoning

1 teaspoon kosher salt

Pepper, freshly ground, to taste

1 stick (½ cup) unsalted butter, melted

Roasted Garlic Aioli (RECIPEA FOLLOWS)

Combine eggs, mayonnaise, and mustard in a medium mixing bowl and stir until well combined. Add bread crumbs and crabmeat, breaking up any large chunks with a fork. Add Old Bay, salt, and pepper, and gently combine all ingredients.

With moistened hands, shape into 1-inch slightly flattened rounds, using about 1 tablespoon of the crab mixture each. Place cakes an inch apart on parchment-covered baking sheets. At this point, you may refrigerate cakes for up to 4 hours, covered with plastic wrap.

When ready to cook, preheat oven to 400°F. Brush each cake lightly with melted butter and bake until crisp and golden, about 15–20 minutes. Serve with Roasted Garlic Aioli or fresh lemon wedges.

Crab cakes can be made a day ahead. Refrigerate the baked, cooled cakes in an airtight container. Reheat for 5 minutes in a preheated 400°F oven.

*Japanese bread crumbs, or *Panko*, can be found in specialty stores or the Asian foods section of many large supermarkets.

MAKES 6 DOZEN HORS D'OEUVRE–SIZED CRAB CAKES

Nesting Ch[

You can make the smoked-salmon dip spicier b[
Blossom horseradish dip. I discovered this sp[
vinegar, and spices in the mustard section of[
found many uses for it. If your gourmet store d[
grated horseradish from the jar. For a quick h[
filling with your favorite cracker or cocktail p[
with a star tip into the baked Wonton Cups on[

2 pints cherry tomatoes

1 8-ounce package cream cheese,
    room temperature

1 8-ounce package good-quality sliced s[
    roughly chopped

2–3 tablespoons Onion Blossom horserad[

Fresh parsley or dill sprigs for garnish

Sprouts for serving (optional)

ROASTED GARLIC AIOLI

1 head of garlic, unpeeled

1 teaspoon olive oil

²/₃ cup mayonnaise

2 tablespoons fresh lemon juice

¼ cup horseradish

¼ teaspoon ground cayenne pepper

Preheat oven to 400°F.

Using a sharp knife, cut about ¾ inch off the pointy end of the garlic head, exposing the cloves. Drizzle the olive oil over the garlic. Wrap the garlic head completely in a piece of aluminum foil and bake for 45 minutes, until tender. When they're cool enough to handle, squeeze the garlic cloves out of their papery skin and into a blender. Puree with mayonnaise, lemon juice, horseradish, and cayenne pepper. Cover and refrigerate aioli up to three days.

MAKES 1 CUP

Jicama Sticks with Fresh Cilantro

Jicama is a Mexican root vegetable that is both crunchy and sweet. The addition of chili powder makes it irresistible. This is a perfect low-fat hors d'oeuvre for a summer cocktail party.

2½–3 pounds jicama

4 tablespoons fresh lime juice

1 teaspoon sugar

1 teaspoon kosher salt

1 teaspoon chili powder

½ cup fresh cilantro, chopped, for garnish

Peel the jicama and cut into horizontal ¼-inch julienne strips. Place in a large bowl and add the lime juice, tossing gently to coat well. In a separate bowl, stir together the sugar, salt, and chili powder. Lay the julienned strips flat on a baking sheet, and sprinkle the chili powder mixture over all sides (a flour sifter works well for this). Chill until ready to serve. To serve, stand the jicama upright in a bowl and garnish with cilantro.

SERVES 12 AS AN HORS D'OEUVRE

Beef Tend

This is a basic roast tenderloin recipe, b
the thinly sliced beef on baguette slices
Horseradish Sauce, and enjoy! Have y
tenderloin for you. Also, find a baguette
that of the tenderloin.

1 2½–3-pound beef tenderloin, trimm
1 tablespoon kosher salt
1 tablespoon pepper, freshly ground
2 tablespoons fresh rosemary, coarse
2 tablespoons olive oil
Baguette, sliced into ¼-inch thick slice
Homemade Horseradish Sauce (RECI

Preheat oven to 450°F.

Place the tenderloin on a foil-lined bakin(
with olive oil. Season with salt and pepper
on the oven's middle rack and bake for
thermometer registers 130°F to 140°F for r
foil, and let rest at least 10–15 minutes be
slices. Place on top of the baguette roun(
of horseradish sauce before serving.

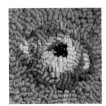

Lemon-Almond Sugar Cookies

The almonds and lemon zest were last-minute additions to this basic sugar-cookie dough. I had a few bags of slivered almonds left over from a different recipe, so I added them to the batter and then dipped the finished cookies in a sugar-and-ground-almond coating. The lemon zest gives the cookie a light and pleasing taste. This dough also freezes well.

¾ cup slivered almonds, plus ¼ cup for coating
1 cup sugar, plus ½ cup for coating
1½ sticks (¾ cup) unsalted butter, softened
1 large egg
¼ teaspoon almond extract
1 tablespoon lemon zest, grated from 1 large lemon
1½ cups flour, plus extra for rolling
¼ teaspoon salt

Preheat oven to 425°F.

Toast the almonds on a parchment-covered baking sheet until golden and fragrant, about 5–7 minutes. Cool completely.

Place ¼ cup almonds and ½ cup sugar in a food processor and process until coarsely chopped. Set aside.

Using a stand or handheld mixer, cream the butter and remaining 1 cup sugar on medium speed in a large mixing bowl until fluffy, about 2 minutes. Add the egg, almond extract, and lemon zest and continue beating on medium speed until well mixed, about 30 seconds. Reduce speed to low and stir in the flour, salt, and remaining almonds, mixing just until a soft dough forms.

Divide the dough in half. Lightly flour the work surface and shape each half into an 8-inch log about 1½ inches in diameter. Cover in plastic wrap and refrigerate at least 2 hours or overnight. (Note: To freeze, wrap tightly in plastic and store in an airtight container for up to two months.)

When ready to bake, preheat oven to 350°F. Using a large, sharp knife, slice rolls into ¼-inch-thick rounds and place an inch apart on ungreased cookie sheets. Bake for 8–10 minutes, or until the edges are very light brown. Remove from the oven and let stand for 1 minute, then remove to wire rack. While still warm, dip each cookie in reserved sugar and almond mixture, completely covering both top and bottom. Cool completely. Store in airtight container for up to one week.

MAKES ABOUT 6 DOZEN

Nonalcoholic Piña Coladas

It's a good idea to offer a nonalcoholic drink at large parties or gatherings, especially when teenagers are invited. This creamy coconut-based drink is refreshing and will be enjoyed by guests of all ages.

4 cups pineapple, cubed from 1 large fresh pineapple

1 15-ounce can coconut cream*

1 46-ounce can pineapple juice, about 6 cups

12 cups ice cubes

1 2-liter bottle ginger ale, chilled

2 10-ounce jars maraschino cherries (optional)

Mix the pineapple chunks, coconut cream, and pineapple juice in a large bowl. Combine 3 cups of the pineapple mixture with 3 cups ice in a blender, and blend until uniform. Repeat with the remaining mixture. Pour into a punch bowl, add ginger ale, and stir to blend. Serve cold, with additional ice if necessary. Garnish each drink with maraschino cherries, if desired.

*Coconut cream can be found in specialty stores or the ethnic section of most large supermarkets.

SERVES 12

CHAPTER THREE *simply stradivarius*

Treble-Clef Caviar Torte

This has become our signature hors d'oeuvre. Each torte is a stunning work of culinary art created by Chef Ed Batejan. Technically, only sturgeon eggs from the Caspian Sea can be classified as caviar; the rest of the world's fish eggs are called roe. While the recipe may at first appear to be an expensive undertaking, it is made economical with the substitution of roe for beluga, osetra, or sevruga caviar. The torte will serve up to seventy-five guests as part of a cocktail party. Guests never want to be the first to cut into the creative designs, but Dale, Susan, and I are always happy to oblige!

Vegetable oil spray

24 large eggs,
    hard-cooked, cooled, peeled, and finely chopped*

1 cup mayonnaise

2 tablespoons Dijon mustard

¼ teaspoon pepper, freshly ground

2 packets (½ ounce) unflavored Knox gelatin

2 cups red caviar, optional

2 cups black lumpfish caviar, to decorate (use any combination
    of black, red, orange, or gold, depending on design)

To prepare the torte pan, spray the sides and bottom of a 12-inch springform pan with vegetable oil spray.

Place chopped eggs in a large mixing bowl. Add the mayonnaise, Dijon mustard, and pepper, mixing well.

Place the gelatin in a small bowl and add 2 tablespoons of cold water, stirring with a fork to combine. Let the gelatin mixture sit for about 3 minutes to thicken. Pour in 2 tablespoons of boiling water, stirring until dissolved. Pour the gelatin mixture over the egg mixture and gently blend until well combined. Mix in the red caviar, if using. Fill the springform pan with the egg mixture and shake gently to settle (or use a spatula to flatten).

Cover with parchment paper or plastic wrap and refrigerate overnight until firm. When ready to decorate, run a small knife around the pan's inside edge. Gently remove the sides and invert the torte onto a large plate.

The torte can be decorated with caviar up to 5 hours before serving. Spread the top and/or sides with caviar, and with a knife, gently smooth to adhere. Cover and refrigerate. Serve with crackers or toast points.

*To hard-cook eggs: Place eggs in a large pot. Add cold water to cover. Bring to a boil, then remove from heat, cover, and let sit for 15 minutes. Drain and rinse under cold water until cool. Peel immediately.

MAKES 1 12-INCH-ROUND TORTE, 1½ INCHES THICK

AMERICAN CAVIAR

Thought to have originated in ancient China, cured fish roe has been popular in foods from the days of early Persia and ancient Greece and Rome. The luxury survived even through the Dark Ages, when sturgeons and their caviar were reserved exclusively for the king.

After settlers of the New World discovered the prolific lake sturgeon, caviar became so abundant that it was given away to encourage drinking in bars and saloons. In more elegant surroundings, such as the New York Waldorf-Astoria, generous servings were presented as the *amuse-bouche*, "little bites that delight," before the elegant meal began.

You can thank Henry Schacht, the German immigrant who started the American caviar industry on the shores of the Delaware River by catching sturgeon and then preserving their roe with German salt. He was soon exporting the caviar to Europe. Surprisingly, over 90 percent of the world's caviar was produced in the United States from the beginning of the nineteenth century until early in the twentieth century, when the once abundant sturgeon had been fished until near-extinction and American production was stopped.

AMERICAN STURGEON

Small pearl-gray grains; an excellent substitute for expensive Russian caviars such as beluga, osetra, and sevruga

WHITEFISH ROE

Pleasant tiny, firm eggs, an almost iridescent pale orange or golden in color; very subtle flavor; also known as American golden caviar, from the Great Lakes golden whitefish

SALMON ROE

Large eggs, glistening orange-red color; mild flavor; from Alaska or the Pacific Northwest

TROUT ROE

Medium-grained roe with what appears to be a tiny orange eye in the center of each egg; bold, quite salty, and slightly sticky; from Great Lakes freshwater trout

LUMPFISH

Black, orange, or red in color; very inexpensive roe from the North American lumpsucker fish

TOBIKKO OR JAPANESE FLYING-FISH ROE

Once used mostly by sushi chefs, this economical, versatile, crunchy, but delicate-grained roe is popular for its brilliant, glittery colors; may be used as a substitute in recipes calling for the more traditional roes; available in a vibrant array of colors and intense flavors: fluorescent orange, brilliant red, dense, velvety black, soft golden horseradish, or wasabi-flavored neon green

Bacon-Wrapped Grissini

This is one of my most requested hors d'oeuvres and a family favorite. I have to hide these or leave a stern note when I'm making them for a party, or they will disappear one by one. I love teaching someone how to carefully roll the soft bacon around the breadstick without breaking too many of them—and even the broken ones go. Just take your time and roll gently; you'll get the hang of it. The smell of chili powder, bacon, and brown sugar baking in your oven is worth rolling all these little breadsticks!

¾ cup packed light brown sugar

3 tablespoons chili powder

1 4½-ounce box thin grissini breadsticks

1 pound thin uncooked bacon, room temperature

Preheat oven to 350°F. Line two heavy baking sheets with aluminum foil.

Place the brown sugar and chili powder in a sifter and sift into a shallow baking sheet long enough for the grissini. Carefully wrap a slice of bacon in a spiral around each breadstick. Set aside on a sheet of foil.

When all breadsticks are wrapped, gently roll each one into the brown sugar mixture, coating the bacon very well. Arrange on the foil-lined baking sheets about half an inch apart. Bake 20 minutes, or until the coating has caramelized and the bacon is well cooked and has shrunk slightly. Immediately remove from the baking sheet with tongs and place on a sheet of foil to cool and firm, about 15 minutes. Bacon will become crisp and breadsticks will harden when they cool. Serve at room temperature.

MAKES ABOUT 2 DOZEN

Pat's Spinach Buttons with Aioli Filling

Ed Batejan's mother, Pat, fills her beef roulade Milanese with this unusual stuffing flavored with spinach, Genoa salami, garlic, rosemary, and Parmesan cheese. Ed served this special recipe at an extraordinary luncheon my Princeton friends gave for my birthday two years ago. After tasting the stuffing, I suggested that he create an hors d'oeuvre. Pat uses unseasoned Italian bread crumbs for her filling, but we dressed up the balls a little by rolling them in crunchy Japanese bread crumbs and then deep-frying them. Ed's garlic mayonnaise is the perfect topping. Thanks, Pat!

1 pound frozen chopped spinach, thawed completely

2 tablespoons extra virgin olive oil

1½ cups (about ⅓ pound) Genoa salami, diced

4 garlic cloves, minced

⅓ cup shallots, finely chopped

2 tablespoons fresh rosemary, finely chopped

¼ cup sherry

½ cup Parmesan cheese, freshly grated

½ cup Italian bread crumbs

2 large eggs

Black pepper, freshly ground, to taste

2 quarts canola or safflower oil, for frying

1½ cups Japanese bread crumbs *

Garlic Aioli Filling (RECIPEA FOLLOWS)

Place the spinach in a strainer and press, removing as much liquid as possible. With paper towels or a dish towel, pat dry—the dryer the spinach, the better it will adhere when frying. Set aside.

CHAPTER FOUR *pins and needles*

Potato-Roquefort Crisps with Red-Pepper Cream

Ann Mann shared this potato-pancake recipe, and I immediately thought it would make a wonderful hors d'oeuvre. We topped these crispy pancakes with a red-pepper cream and small bites of Roquefort cheese. They are equally delicious as a side dish with beef or chicken.

1¼ pounds peeled Yukon Gold potatoes,
    cut into 1-inch chunks (about 2½ cups)

2 cloves garlic, minced

2 tablespoons unsalted butter, chilled

4 ounces Roquefort blue cheese, crumbled

1 tablespoon fresh chives, finely chopped

1 tablespoon shallots, minced

½ teaspoon salt

½ teaspoon pepper, freshly ground

2 tablespoons unsalted butter, melted

⅓ cup bread crumbs

1 tablespoon parsley, finely chopped

Vegetable oil spray or olive oil

Red Pepper Cream (RECIPEA FOLLOWS)

Place the potatoes and garlic in a small saucepan and add cold water to cover. Bring to a boil. Cook about 10 minutes, or until the potatoes are tender when pierced with a fork. Drain and mash in a large bowl with a potato masher or large fork. Add the cold butter, 2 tablespoons of the blue cheese, chives, shallots, salt, and pepper. Mix well. For hors d'oeuvres, use a measuring tablespoon to form the potato mixture into small pancakes about 2 inches in diameter, using your palm to flatten them slightly. Place pancakes on waxed-paper-lined baking sheets, alternating layers of waxed paper and pancakes. Cover and refrigerate for at least 4 hours, or overnight.

To cook, preheat oven to 425°F. Spray a baking sheet lightly with vegetable oil, or brush lightly with olive oil. Mix the bread crumbs and parsley and set aside. Carefully peel the pancakes off the waxed paper and place about 1 inch apart on the baking sheet. Brush each pancake with melted butter and sprinkle with the bread-crumb mixture. Bake for about 15 minutes, or until golden brown and crisp. Serve warm, topped with small dollops of red-pepper cream and the remaining crumbled Roquefort cheese.

SERVES 12 AS AN HORS D'OEUVRE

RED PEPPER CREAM

1 cup roasted red peppers, drained and coarsely chopped

½ cup sour cream

2 cloves garlic, minced

1 teaspoon fresh lemon juice

2 tablespoons Dijon mustard

1 teaspoon fresh chives, chopped

Salt and freshly ground pepper to taste

Place first six ingredients in a blender and puree until well blended. Season to taste with salt and pepper. Chill 1–2 hours before serving. Whisk until creamy, and use a small spoon or plastic squeeze bottle to dress each pancake with a bit of sauce.

MAKES ABOUT 1½ CUPS

Saffron-Infused Scallops with Golden Crème Fraîche

When prepared this way, scallops melt in your mouth. The saffron and white-wine poaching liquid transform these already delicate bites into golden morsels. Saffron crème fraîche is the perfect final touch.

> 1 bottle good-quality dry white wine
>
> 1 teaspoon saffron threads, plus more for garnish if desired
>
> 1 bay leaf
>
> 1 pound sea scallops (about 2 dozen)
>
> ¼ cup paprika
>
> Salt and freshly ground pepper to taste
>
> 4 tablespoons extra virgin olive oil, divided
>
> Wooden toothpicks for serving
>
> Golden Crème Fraîche (RECIPEA FOLLOWS)

Pour the white wine into a medium heavy saucepan. Crush the saffron between your fingers, then add it and the bay leaf to the wine. Bring to a boil, then reduce heat to medium and boil until reduced by half, about 15 minutes. Lower heat to a simmer and poach the scallops in liquid, a few at a time, for 30 seconds. Remove with a slotted spoon and place on a paper-towel-lined platter. When all the scallops are poached, bring the liquid back to a boil and reduce sauce by half once again, about another 15 minutes. Remove from heat and reserve for Golden Crème Fraîche.

Gently blot the scallops with paper towels until dry.

To cook, place the paprika in a shallow dish. Press the top and bottom of each scallop into the paprika, leaving the sides uncoated. Season the scallops with salt and pepper. Heat 2 tablespoons olive oil in a medium sauté pan over medium-high heat. When the oil is hot, quickly sear the scallops for approximately 1–2 minutes per side, turning carefully with tongs. Remove scallops to a warm plate, wipe out the pan, and repeat with the remaining olive oil and scallops. Scallops can be served immediately, or prepared to this point and refrigerated overnight, covered. Do not overcook, or they will become tough.

When ready to serve, preheat oven to 350° F. Place the seared scallops on a parchment-covered baking sheet and bake for approximately 5–8 minutes, or until warmed through. To serve, top each scallop with a small amount of Golden Crème Fraîche and, if desired, dust with saffron threads. Insert a toothpick into each scallop.

SERVES 12 AS AN HORS D'OEUVRE

GOLDEN CRÈME FRAÎCHE

> 1 cup crème fraîche or sour cream
>
> 1 or 2 tablespoons scallop poaching liquid, cooled
>
> Salt to taste

In a small glass bowl, mix crème fraîche and 1 tablespoon of the cooled saffron poaching liquid until blended. Season to taste with salt and add additional liquid, if desired. Refrigerate for at least one hour or until serving time.

MAKES 1 CUP

Chipotle Chicken Sates with Cilantro Cream

This is a real crowd pleaser. I am a big fan of spicy foods, and the combination of chipotle chiles and cayenne provides a wonderful flavor. These sates definitely have a bite to them, though the cilantro cream cools the burn while adding another layer of flavor. But don't skip this recipe just because you don't like spicy food! Adjust the chili powder and chipotle en adobo accordingly and enjoy a milder but equally delicious chicken sate.

1 8-ounce can chipotle en adobo*

2 pounds boneless, skinless chicken breast halves

24 6-inch wooden skewers, soaked in warm water for 30 minutes

½ cup Japanese bread crumbs*

2 tablespoons Mexican-style chili powder, or to taste

½ teaspoon salt

1 teaspoon black pepper

½ teaspoon cayenne pepper

1 stick unsalted butter, melted

In a food processor or blender, puree the chipotle peppers. Cut the chicken breasts lengthwise into long, thin strips approximately ½ inch thick. Place in a medium bowl and mix in the chipotle peppers. Cover and refrigerate for at least 2 hours or overnight.

In a shallow pan, combine the bread crumbs, Mexican chili powder, salt, black pepper, and cayenne pepper. Set aside.

To cook, thread the chicken strips onto a wooden skewer in a zigzag pattern, leaving about an inch or two exposed at each end. Brush the chicken strips with melted butter and gently roll in the bread-crumb mixture. Place in a single layer on lightly greased or parchment-lined baking sheets. Sprinkle any excess bread crumbs over the sates. Refrigerate, tightly covered with plastic wrap, for one hour. Skewers can be prepared to this point, covered tightly, and refrigerated overnight.

Preheat oven to 400°F. Bake for 8–10 minutes or until crisp and golden brown. Turn once while baking to avoid burning, or cover the exposed wood tips with a small strip of aluminum foil. Serve sates warm with Cilantro Cream.

*Chipotle en adobo and Japanese bread crumbs, or Panko, can be found in specialty stores or in the ethnic section of many large supermarkets.

SERVES 12 AS AN HORS D'OEUVRE

CILANTRO CREAM

2 cups sour cream

½ cup fresh cilantro, chopped

2 tablespoons fresh lime juice

½ teaspoon cumin powder

Salt to taste

Stir together all ingredients in a small serving bowl. Cover and refrigerate until ready to serve. Garnish with a sprig of fresh cilantro and serve in a hollowed-out dried ancho chile or any fresh Mexican green pepper for a fun Tex-Mex presentation.

MAKES 2 CUPS

Noodle-Wrapped Shrimp with Thai Chili Dipping Sauce

Ed Batejan included this recipe at his winter cooking class, held at the Miele U.S. headquarters in Princeton. Served with a spicy Thai dipping sauce, the pasta-wrapped shrimp are an interesting and elegant hors d'oeuvre.

Designed by renowned architect and local Princeton resident Michael Graves, the Miele showroom provides area cooks with dream kitchens full of contemporary stainless ovens, dishwashers, and sleek but incredibly functional European-style cooktops. A gourmet cook's dream, these spaces would inspire any food lover to immediately renovate.

24 large (about 1½ pounds) shrimp,
    peeled and deveined, tails left on
½ pound angel-hair pasta
4 large eggs, lightly beaten
3 green onions, white part only, diced
¾ cup Parmesan cheese, grated
2 teaspoons salt, divided
1 teaspoon pepper, freshly ground, divided
1 teaspoon cayenne pepper, divided
½ cup flour
2 quarts cups peanut or safflower oil
    for deep-frying
Thai Chili Dipping Sauce (RECIPEA FOLLOWS)

Keeping the strands whole, cook the angel-hair pasta according to package instructions until al dente. Drain and rinse in cold water. Set aside.

In a medium bowl, mix the eggs, green onions, cheese, and half each of the salt, pepper, and cayenne. Add the pasta. Toss with your hands until the ingredients are well mixed.

In a small bowl, combine the flour and the remaining salt, pepper, and cayenne. One at a time, coat the shrimp with flour, then wrap well with the pasta mixture, winding gently around each shrimp and leaving the tails exposed. Place the wrapped shrimp on a parchment-lined baking sheet and continue until all are wrapped. Recipe can be prepared one day ahead to this point. Cover tightly with plastic wrap and refrigerate for a few hours until very firm, or freeze for about 30 minutes.

When ready to serve, heat the oil in a 3-quart saucepan or deep fryer to 350°F. Fry the shrimp a few at a time until golden, approximately 1–2 minutes, or until shrimp are pink and noodles are golden brown. (Note: If the pasta loosens when frying, chill again until completely firm.) Carefully remove from the pan with a slotted spoon and drain on paper towels. Sprinkle with salt immediately, if desired. Allow the oil to return to 350°F between each batch. Serve warm with Thai Chili Dipping Sauce.

SERVES 12 AS AN HORS D'OEUVRE

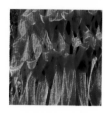

Kathleen's Spiced Pecans

THAI CHILI DIPPING SAUCE

2 tablespoons light brown sugar

2 tablespoons lime juice

2 tablespoons fish sauce

1 tablespoon water

1 tablespoon Thai chili-garlic sauce*

⅓ cup carrot, grated in a food processor

2 garlic cloves, minced

2 tablespoons cilantro, chopped

1 tablespoon hot Thai or Bird's Eye chili pepper, finely chopped

In a small serving bowl, mix the brown sugar, lime juice, fish sauce, water, and chili-garlic sauce. Add the carrot, garlic, cilantro, and chili pepper. Let stand 15 minutes. Serve as a dipping sauce for noodle-wrapped shrimp. May be prepared one day ahead.

 *Thai chili-garlic sauce, also known as sriracha, can be found in specialty stores or the Asian section of many large supermarkets.

MAKES 1 CUP

Warning: These are extremely addictive—freeze to avoid prolonged contact.

½ teaspoon garlic salt

½ teaspoon curry powder

½ teaspoon chili powder

¼ teaspoon ground ginger

¼ teaspoon ground allspice

¼ teaspoon cinnamon

½ teaspoon ground cumin

¼ teaspoon cayenne pepper

1 large egg white

¼ cup sugar

3 cups pecan halves

Preheat oven to 300°F.

Combine the spices in a small bowl and set aside.

In a medium bowl, gently whisk the egg white with sugar until just blended. Stir the dry ingredients into the egg mixture. Add the pecans and gently toss until well coated. Spread evenly in a single layer on an ungreased baking sheet. Bake for 15 minutes. Remove from the oven, stir and separate the nuts. Bake for an additional 10 minutes. Stir the nuts a second time and bake for another 10 minutes, for a total of 35 minutes. The pecans will be a deep chocolate-brown color. Remove the nuts from the oven, spread in a single layer on waxed paper, and cool completely.

MAKES 3 CUPS

CHAPTER FIVE *digging dog farm*

Caramelized Shrimp Wrapped in Bacon

This popular hors d'oeuvre couldn't be easier to make—just wrap bacon around fresh shrimp, roll them in a mixture of sugar and spices, and bake! The result is a sweet and piquant taste that is wonderful either hot or at room temperature.

½ cup sugar

½ cup light brown sugar

1 large clove garlic, minced

1 tablespoon fresh ginger, minced

1 teaspoon salt

½ teaspoon pepper, freshly ground

½ teaspoon cayenne pepper

¼ teaspoon curry

½ teaspoon cinnamon

1 tablespoon flour

24 large shrimp (about 1 pound), peeled and deveined,
    tails intact

12 slices uncooked bacon,
    softened to room temperature and cut in half

Toothpicks, for securing bacon

Preheat oven to 450°F.

In a small mixing bowl, mix both the sugars, the garlic, ginger, salt, pepper, cayenne, curry, cinnamon, and flour. Line a rimmed baking sheet with aluminum foil or parchment paper. Wrap each shrimp with a piece of softened bacon and secure with a toothpick. With your hands, individually coat the shrimp in the sugar mixture, and place on the baking sheet. The shrimp can be prepared ahead to this point. Cover and refrigerate for up to 4 hours.

Bake the shrimp until the bacon is crisp and the sugar is caramelized, about 10–12 minutes. Remove from the oven and immediately place the shrimp on a separate sheet of foil or parchment paper to harden. Serve warm or at room temperature. To reheat, place in a 400°F oven for about 5 minutes.

SERVES 12 AS AN HORS D'OEUVRE

Brie Toasts with Caramelized Pepper-and-Onion Chutney

You'll be amazed by how easy it is to make your own chutney, and how rewarding: The delectable smell of the caramelized peppers and onions fills the house. This chutney is an excellent filler for a puff-pastry-wrapped baked Brie, but it is also a tasty condiment to serve with most soft cheeses, such as a goat cheese or Camembert.

Caramelized Pepper-and-Onion Chutney (RECIPEA FOLLOWS)*

2 12–14-inch sourdough baguettes

½ pound Brie, sliced ¼ inch thick

2 tablespoons fresh chives, chopped, for garnish

Preheat oven to 350°F.

Slice the baguettes into 24 ¼-inch-thick rounds and place on a baking sheet. Bake until lightly toasted and just beginning to color, about 4–5 minutes. Toasts can be prepared ahead and placed in an airtight container for up to a week or frozen for up to a month.

Top each toast with a small slice of Brie, trimmed of white rind if desired. Bake for about 5 minutes, or just until the cheese begins to melt. Remove from oven and top each toast with 1 teaspoon of chutney. Garnish with chives and serve warm.

*You may substitute your favorite store-bought chutney.

SERVES 12 AS AN HORS D'OEUVRE

CARAMELIZED PEPPER-AND-ONION CHUTNEY

¼ cup extra virgin olive oil

2 tablespoons balsamic vinegar

4 large onions, sliced into ½-inch-thick rounds

4 garlic cloves, thinly sliced

4 red bell peppers, sliced into ½-inch strips, seeds and ribs removed

2 packed tablespoons brown sugar

Salt and freshly ground pepper to taste

Heat a large soup pot over medium heat. Add the olive oil and balsamic vinegar. When hot, add the onions, garlic, and red peppers. Cook over medium heat for 30 minutes, stirring occasionally, until soft and beginning to brown. Place in a food processor and pulse just until coarsely chopped. Return to the pot and add the brown sugar, salt, and pepper. Continue to cook over low heat, stirring often, until all liquid has evaporated and the mixture is thick, about 10 minutes. Cool. Chutney can be prepared ahead and refrigerated in a sealed container for up to 2 weeks. Serve at room temperature.

MAKES ABOUT 6 CUPS

Asparagus Gnocchi with Sage and Browned Butter Sauce

For this delicious first course we purchased fresh gnocchi stuffed with asparagus and ricotta cheese, then tossed it with browned butter, fresh sage, and lemon sauce. Check the frozen section of your local supermarket or gourmet store for other varieties of gnocchi, or substitute a favorite tortellini or ravioli. Garnish each serving with blanched asparagus tips, Parmesan-cheese curls, and lemon zest for a combination of flavors that is both aromatic and pleasing to the palate.

    3 pounds (approximately 36 large pieces) fresh or frozen gnocchi

    36 asparagus-spear tips, blanched

    Browned Butter Sauce (RECIPEA FOLLOWS)

    Parmesan-Reggiano cheese, for garnish

    Lemon zest, for garnish

Cook the asparagus tips in boiling water for 4 minutes. Drain and plunge immediately into a bowl of ice water to halt the cooking. Drain again. Asparagus tips can be cooked a day ahead and sealed in a plastic bag lined with paper towels, then refrigerated.

Prepare pasta according to package directions. Place 3 pieces of pasta on each plate and garnish with asparagus tips. Drizzle Browned Butter Sauce over the pasta and garnish with freshly grated or shaved Parmesan cheese and lemon zest.

SERVES 12 AS A FIRST COURSE

BROWNED BUTTER SAUCE

    3 sticks unsalted butter

    3 tablespoons fresh sage, coarsely chopped

    2 tablespoons lemon juice, freshly squeezed

Melt the butter in a heavy saucepan over medium heat, and cook until the solids begin to brown, about 5–10 minutes. Remove from heat and stir in the sage and lemon juice.

Use immediately.

MAKES ABOUT 1½ CUPS

Mesclun Greens
with Warmed Goat Cheese and Maple-Dijon Vinaigrette

Warmed goat-cheese rounds atop salad greens are always an elegant touch at a dinner party. But when dressed with this sweet vinaigrette, made with maple syrup and Dijon mustard, they become a special treat. Kathleen Gittleman shared the vinaigrette recipe and told me that her kids would eat it with a spoon if she let them. After one batch, I was also hooked. The vinaigrette keeps for weeks, never separates, and adds just the right amount of sweetness to any salad combination. The pepper and shallots add a depth of flavors that your guests will find intriguing.

1½ cups toasted walnuts,

    finely chopped, from 2 cups whole walnuts

2 10.5-ounce fresh goat-cheese logs

3 large egg yolks

⅓ cup water

1½ cups fresh bread crumbs

¼–½ cup extra virgin olive oil

12 ounces mesclun salad greens

1 pint grape tomatoes

1 large red onion, thinly sliced

Maple-Dijon Vinaigrette (RECIPEA FOLLOWS)

Salt and freshly ground pepper to taste

Preheat oven to 350°F.

To toast the walnuts, spread them on a parchment-lined baking sheet and bake until lightly browned and fragrant, about 5–10 minutes. Remove and cool completely. Place in a food processor and chop finely.

Slice the goat cheese into 36 rounds, approximately ¼ inch thick. In a small bowl, whisk the egg yolks and water. In another small bowl, mix the bread crumbs and toasted nuts. Dunk the cheese rounds in the egg mixture, then dip them in the bread crumbs, pressing gently to coat on all sides. Place the cheese rounds on a parchment-lined baking sheet and chill, covered with plastic wrap, for at least 1 hour or overnight. Goat-cheese rounds may be chilled in the refrigerator and then frozen between layers of waxed paper in a plastic container for up to 1 week. Do not thaw before cooking.

When ready to serve, heat 2 tablespoons of the olive oil in a large heavy sauté pan over medium heat. Cook the coated cheese rounds just until the outside is crisp and golden, about 2 minutes per side, or 3 minutes if frozen. Wipe out the pan, add another 2 tablespoons of the oil, and continue until all the cheese rounds are cooked. Keep warm in a 200°F oven until ready to serve.

In a large salad bowl, combine the salad greens, tomatoes, and sliced red onions, and toss with vinaigrette to taste. Divide the salad onto plates, and top each serving with 3 rounds of warmed goat cheese. Season with salt and pepper. Serve immediately.

SERVES 12

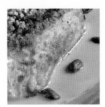

Pistachio-Crusted Halibut with Champagne Cream Sauce

MAPLE-DIJON VINAIGRETTE

¾ cup vegetable oil

¼ cup red wine vinegar

2 cloves garlic, finely chopped

¼ cup shallots, finely chopped

½ teaspoon black pepper, freshly ground

¼ cup Dijon mustard

½ cup good-quality maple syrup

Salt to taste

Whisk all ingredients in a small bowl until combined. May be made ahead and stored in a sealed jar for up to a month. Shake well before using.

MAKES 2 CUPS

I usually select sea bass or mahimahi for dinner parties, but when I discussed this menu with Chef Ed Batejan, he urged me to try his baked halibut with a pistachio crust. The soft, buttery flavor of this fish was a perfect match for the pistachio and bread-crumb topping. As a treat for Anne and her guests, we added a champagne and pistachio cream sauce, the perfect complement to the halibut. Pistachios and champagne—who would have thought!

1½ sticks unsalted butter

6 large shallots, chopped

2 cups peeled unsalted raw pistachio nuts,
    coarsely chopped

1 cup dry white wine, divided

2 cups Japanese bread crumbs*

6 tablespoons chives, chopped

Salt and freshly ground pepper to taste

12 4-ounce halibut fillets, with skin

Champagne Cream Sauce (RECIPEA FOLLOWS)

Melt ½ stick of butter over medium heat in a medium sauté pan. Add the shallots and cook, stirring, until golden, about 10 minutes. Stir in the pistachios and continue to cook until the nuts are toasted and golden brown, another 3–5 minutes. Add ½ cup of the white wine and stir, scraping any browned bits off the bottom of the pan. Remove from heat and add the bread crumbs and chives. Season with salt and pepper. Set aside to cool slightly before coating fish, or cover and refrigerate for up to 4 hours.

Preheat oven to 400°F.

Place the fish pieces an inch apart on a large parchment-lined, rimmed baking sheet. Melt the remaining stick of butter and brush over each halibut piece. Reserve any remaining butter to drizzle on top of the fish after bread-crumb mixture is added. Season with salt and pepper. Press about ¼ cup of the bread-crumb mixture on top of each piece of fish. Add the remaining ½ cup of white wine to the pan and cover with foil.

Bake the fish for 15–18 minutes or until cooked through. Raise the oven temperature to 450°F. Remove the foil and cook for an additional 3–5 minutes or until the top is crisp and light brown. Using a spatula, remove the fish from the pan, leaving the skin behind. Serve with Champagne Cream Sauce.

*Japanese bread crumbs, or Panko, can be found in specialty stores or the Asian section of many large supermarkets.

SERVES 12

CHAMPAGNE CREAM SAUCE

1 stick plus 3 tablespoons unsalted butter

6 medium leeks, sliced
(white and pale green part only)

1 bottle good-quality brut champagne

3 cups heavy cream

Salt and white pepper to taste

½ cup unsalted pistachio pieces

Melt the stick of butter in a large heavy saucepan over medium heat. Add the leeks and cook, stirring often, until tender but not brown, about 20 minutes. Add the champagne and bring to a boil. Boil until the liquid is reduced, about 15 minutes. Pour the liquid through a strainer, pressing to release all the juice, then discard the leeks.

Return the liquid to the saucepan and add the heavy cream. Bring to a simmer over medium heat and reduce by half again, about 40–45 minutes. (The sauce should be thick enough to coat the back of a spoon.) Remove from heat and whisk in the remaining 3 tablespoons of butter until smooth. Season to taste with salt and white pepper. Serve with Pistachio-Crusted Halibut. Spoon a few tablespoons of sauce on plate and place the fish on top. Garnish with pistachio pieces.

MAKES 3 CUPS

Roasted Baby Vegetables

Purple and Gold Roasted Fingerling Potatoes

You can use any combination of your favorite seasonal vegetables in this recipe. Be sure to vary the colors so the visual treat is as exciting as the taste.

1 pound baby carrots

1 pound baby zucchini, trimmed

½ pound baby pattypan squash, halved

½ pound brussels sprouts, halved

1 stick unsalted butter, melted

Salt and freshly ground pepper to taste

Cook the baby carrots in salted boiling water for 2 minutes. Drain and rinse in cold water until cooled. Drain well and pat dry.

Combine all the vegetables in a large bowl. Drizzle with melted butter and toss thoroughly to coat. The vegetables can be prepared to this point 2 hours ahead. Cover and let stand at room temperature.

Preheat oven to 400°F. Spread the vegetable mixture on a large heavy baking sheet. Season with salt and pepper. Roast until tender and slightly caramelized or golden brown, stirring occasionally, about 30–40 minutes. Serve immediately.

SERVES 12

This recipe would work with any combination of potatoes, but the soft gold and purple of the fingerlings was striking against the hand-painted plates selected for this table. Anne's party was about mixing colors, designs, and textures. This side dish was a visually pleasing ornament to the delicate Pistachio-Crusted Halibut with Champagne Cream Sauce.

Vegetable oil spray

1½ pounds small Yukon Gold fingerling potatoes

1½ pounds small purple fingerling potatoes

2 cups small whole shallots, peeled

10 medium whole garlic cloves, peeled

4 tablespoons olive oil

Salt and freshly ground pepper to taste

3 tablespoons fresh rosemary, chopped

Preheat oven to 400°F. Spray a baking sheet with vegetable oil spray.

Cut the potatoes into 1-inch rounds. In a large bowl, toss the potatoes, shallots, and garlic cloves with olive oil. Season with salt, pepper, and rosemary. Spread the potatoes on a baking sheet and roast for 45–50 minutes, stirring occasionally, until the potatoes are tender and golden brown and the shallots and garlic are soft and caramelized.

To make ahead, let the potatoes cool to room temperature after roasting. Reheat in a 400°F oven for 5–10 minutes, or until warmed through.

SERVES 12

Lemon-Butter Dinner Rolls Baked in Terra-Cotta Pots

Inexpensive terra-cotta pots from the local craft store were filled with a fragrant and buttery dinner roll for an element of fun on our table setting in the hundred-year-old barn. This idea would work with almost any yeast bread recipe; just be sure to follow the simple instructions for preparing the pots.

12 3-inch terra-cotta pots

Vegetable oil spray

1 envelope active dry yeast

⅛ teaspoon sugar

½ cup warm water (105°F to 115°F)

¾ cup warm 2 percent or whole milk (105°F to 115°F)

1 stick unsalted butter, melted

1 large egg

1 large egg yolk

2 packed tablespoons lemon zest,
     plus 2 additional packed teaspoons for lemon butter

2 teaspoons salt

4 cups all-purpose flour,
     plus extra (up to ¼ cup) for kneading

4 tablespoons unsalted butter for lemon butter,
     plus 1 additional tablespoon for greasing bowl

TO PREPARE FLOWERPOTS

Preheat oven to 450°F.

Wash the pots well with hot water, and place on paper towels or a drying rack. When they're thoroughly dry, coat the inside with a thin layer of vegetable oil spray, then wipe out the excess with paper towels. Bake on the middle oven rack for 30 minutes (the oven may smoke slightly). Remove the pots to a rack and cool completely before first use. After each use, wipe well with paper towels, but do not wash.

TO PREPARE ROLLS

Sprinkle the yeast and sugar over warm water in a small bowl. Stir to dissolve. Let stand until foamy, about 10 minutes.

In the bowl of a heavy-duty mixer fitted with the paddle attachment, combine the warm milk, melted butter, egg and egg yolk, 2 tablespoons of the lemon zest, and salt. Add the yeast mixture and 2 cups of flour. Mix on medium-low speed until smooth and creamy, about 2–3 minutes. Add the remaining flour on low speed ½ cup at a time until a soft dough forms; scrape down the sides of the bowl as needed. Scrape the dough onto a lightly floured surface and knead until smooth and elastic, adding more flour as needed, for 5–6 minutes. (If you prefer, use the dough hook attachment on your mixer to knead the dough at medium speed.)

Grease a large mixing bowl with the tablespoon of softened butter. Add the dough, turning to coat the entire surface. Cover the bowl with a dish towel and let rise until double in bulk, about 1¼–1½ hours.

To make the lemon butter, melt 4 tablespoons of unsalted butter with the remaining 2 teaspoons of lemon zest in a small saucepan over low heat. Set aside.

Spray the insides of the flowerpots generously with vegetable oil. Set aside.

When the dough has doubled, punch down with your fist and place on a lightly floured work surface. Knead briefly until smooth. Divide the dough into 12 equal pieces (cover with plastic wrap to prevent drying out while you're working). Divide each piece of dough into 3 equal parts and roll each into a smooth ball. Place 3 small balls in each prepared flowerpot. Cover the pots loosely with dish towels and let rise in a warm draft-free area until doubled, about 35–40 minutes.

Position a rack in the middle of the oven and preheat to 350°F.

Brush the tops of the rolls generously with warm lemon butter. Bake until golden brown, about 20-25 minutes. Rolls can be warmed in a preheated 400°F oven for 5 minutes before serving.

MAKES 12 3-INCH POTS (36 ROLLS)

White-Chocolate Satin Tarts with Glazed Fresh Raspberries

Filled with layers of raspberry and satiny-smooth white-chocolate fillings, then topped with glazed fresh raspberries, these individual tarts are impressive but easy to make ahead. You'll find numerous uses for Annie B's ultra-reliable 3-2-1 Dough. The name comes from the proportion of flour to butter to sugar, by weight, used in her bakery recipe. If you're baking for a crowd, these recipes can easily be doubled.

12 4-inch-round-by-½-inch-deep baked individual tart shells
     made with 3-2-1 Dough (RECIPEA FOLLOWS)
1½ cups Raspberry Base (RECIPEA FOLLOWS)
2 cups White-Chocolate Satin (RECIPEA FOLLOWS)
Fresh raspberries, for garnish
½ cup seedless apricot jam
2 tablespoons water
Raspberry coulis, optional

Fill each cooled tart shell with 1½ tablespoons of the warm Raspberry Base. Freeze for 30 minutes, or until the Raspberry Base is firm. Then fill the remainder of the shells with 2–3 tablespoons of White-Chocolate Satin, rotating each tart slightly to encourage the chocolate to completely cover the Raspberry Base. Freeze until set. (For longer storage, wrap the undecorated tarts well, place in an airtight container, and freeze for up to a month.)

Remove the tarts from the freezer fifteen minutes before serving. Top with the fresh raspberries. To glaze the raspberries, melt the apricot jam with the water over low heat in a small saucepan, stirring until smooth. Using a small

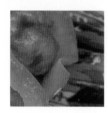

Glazed Yellowfin Tuna Bites in Wonton Cups

You will need miniature-muffin pans to prepare these tiny wonton cups. Once you make them, they're certain to become part of your party repertoire. Baked, they are the perfect base for herbed cheese or crab, lobster, or chicken salad. We filled them with small bites of glazed yellowfin tuna, garnished with pickled ginger slices. Think of these crispy golden treats as the Asian version of our crusty French bread rounds.

1 pound fresh yellowfin tuna steaks, finely chopped

2 tablespoons Dijon mustard

2 cloves garlic, minced

¼ cup scallions, finely chopped

¼ cup red pepper, finely chopped

1 tablespoon fresh ginger, minced

¼ teaspoon cayenne pepper

½ teaspoon salt

¼ teaspoon black pepper, freshly ground

Vegetable oil spray

Pickled ginger slices for garnish

Wonton Cups (RECIPEA FOLLOWS)

Asian Citrus Glaze (RECIPEA FOLLOWS)

Preheat oven to 400°F.

TO MAKE TUNA BITES

Chop the tuna into 2-inch pieces. Pulse briefly in a food processor, just until the coarsely chopped tuna resembles ground beef or pork. Remove any white sinew that sticks to the blade. Place the ground tuna in a medium mixing bowl and add the mustard, garlic, scallions, red pepper, ginger, cayenne pepper, salt, and black pepper. Mix thoroughly. Cover with plastic wrap and refrigerate for at least an hour or overnight.

To prepare, line a baking sheet with parchment paper. Spray lightly with vegetable oil. With wet hands, form the ground tuna into small balls, about 1 teaspoon each. Place on prepared baking sheet.

Brush the tuna bites generously with Asian Citrus Glaze and bake until just cooked through, about 4–5 minutes. Remove from the oven and brush again with warm reserved glaze (for sanitary reasons, be sure to use a different brush). Place a tuna bite in each wonton cup and garnish with thin slices of pickled ginger. Serve warm or at room temperature.

SERVES 12

WONTON CUPS

1 12-ounce package 3-inch wonton wrappers

Vegetable oil or spray

Preheat oven to 325°F.

Cut each wonton square into four small squares. Brush or spray lightly with vegetable oil. Press gently into miniature-muffin tins, oiled side down. Bake until light golden, 5–10 minutes. (Watch carefully, the baking time may decrease for successive batches as the pans heat up.) Cool completely on a wire rack. Cups can be made 3 days in advance and stored in an airtight container at room temperature, or frozen for up to a month

MAKES 6 DOZEN APPETIZER-SIZED CUPS

Shrimp Tempura with Tentsuyu Dipping Sauce

ASIAN CITRUS GLAZE

2 cups fresh orange juice

3 tablespoons fresh lemon juice

2 tablespoons fresh lime juice

¾ cup soy sauce or tamari

1 tablespoon balsamic vinegar

1 tablespoon toasted sesame oil

⅓ cup fresh ginger, peeled and chopped

Combine all ingredients in a small heavy saucepan. Bring to a boil over high heat, stirring constantly. Reduce heat to medium and simmer for 30–45 minutes, stirring occasionally, until the glaze coats the back of a spoon. Pour the sauce through a fine strainer into a bowl. Cover and refrigerate for up to a week. Reheat before using as glaze.

Note: Sauce is best made a day ahead to allow the flavors to blend.

MAKES 2 CUPS

Tempura dates back to the fifteenth century and was introduced to the Japanese by Portuguese and Dutch traders. Its popularity didn't grow, however, until the seventeenth century, when street merchants started selling deep-fried shrimp fresh from Tokyo Bay. Tempura quickly became Japan's version of a fast-food snack. Today both fresh fish and vegetables are dipped into a batter and then deep-fried. The secret to the crisp coating, or cloak (called *koromo*), is a lumpy batter made with cold ingredients and a constant oil temperature. In Japan, tempura is served immediately after frying with either tentsuyu dipping sauce or coarse salt and fresh lemon.

2 pounds large shrimp (about 50), peeled and deveined, tails left on

3 quarts peanut or vegetable oil

2 cups ice cubes for ice bath

2 cups club soda, chilled

1 large egg

2 tablespoons kosher salt

2 cups cake flour, plus 2 tablespoons

Tentsuyu Dipping Sauce (RECIPEA FOLLOWS)

Preheat oil in a wok or deep fryer to 360°F.*

Lay the shrimp flat and make several small diagonal incisions on each side, stretching the body out to prevent curling when frying. Thoroughly dry the shrimp with paper towels and refrigerate.

Fill a mixing bowl halfway with ice. Immediately before frying, mix the club soda, egg, and salt in a slightly larger mixing bowl. Add the cake flour and whisk quickly with chopsticks or a fork until just moistened. Batter should remain slightly lumpy. Place the batter bowl on top of the ice to keep the mixture chilled.

Holding the tail, dip each shrimp in the batter and then place directly in the hot oil. Deep-fry a few shrimp at a time for about 3 minutes, until the shrimp are pink and the tempura batter is crispy and lightly browned. Remove from oil with a slotted spoon and drain on a wire rack set over paper towels. Serve hot with Tentsuyu Dipping Sauce.

*To test for the correct frying temperature, drop a small amount of batter into the hot oil. If it floats back up to the surface, the oil is approximately 360°F and ready to use (adding the shrimp will lower the temperature). If the batter drops to the bottom, the oil is not hot enough. The perfect temperature is 350°F for shrimp and 340°F for vegetables. To prevent burning, skim off any bits of batter that may accumulate at the top of the oil. Fry in small batches and maintain the proper oil temperature to assure a crisp, non-oily coating.

Vegetables such as snap peas, green beans, green peppers, mushrooms, eggplant, and sweet potatoes can also be fried in the batter. Thinly slice large vegetables so they cook through.

SERVES 12

TENTSUYU DIPPING SAUCE

This sauce is traditionally served with sweet grated daikon radish and fresh ginger. When eating tempura as a main course, guests add the desired amount of sauce to individual portions. The base is *dashi-no-moto*, a granular fish soup stock made from dried bonito tuna flakes. *Dashi* is sold in powdered form and is reconstituted with boiling water.

1 cup water
½ teaspoon *dashi-no-moto**
⅓ cup mirin or sake*
⅓ cup soy sauce
¼ cup daikon radish, grated
1 teaspoon fresh ginger, grated

Bring water to a boil in a small saucepan and add *dashi-no-moto*. Boil for three minutes. Remove from heat and stir in the mirin or sake and the soy sauce. Transfer to a bowl. (The sauce can be made several days ahead. Cover and refrigerate.) Add grated daikon radish and ginger before serving.

*Can be found in specialty stores or the Asian section of many large supermarkets.

MAKES 1¼ CUPS

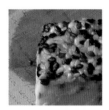

Sesame Salmon Squares with Lemon-Miso Sauce

Find a thick cut of salmon for this recipe, from the part of the fish closest to the head, so that the squares are all roughly the same height. Preparation is surprisingly simple; each piece of fish gets a quick coating of egg white and a dip in black and white sesame seeds. Visit your Asian market or the ethnic foods section at your grocery store for black sesame seeds, mirin, and miso. The miso we use is often labeled white but has a yellow tint.

¼ cup black sesame seeds

¼ cup white sesame seeds

1½ pounds salmon fillet, skinned, boned,
    and cut into 1-inch-square pieces

Kosher salt and freshly ground pepper to taste

2 large egg whites

Cocktail toothpicks

Lemon-Miso Sauce (RECIPEA FOLLOWS)

Preheat oven to 400°F.

On a large plate, mix the sesame seeds; set aside. Line a large baking sheet with foil or parchment paper.

Season the salmon cubes with salt and pepper. Whisk the egg whites until frothy. Taking care not to cover the sides or bottom of the squares, dunk the top into the egg whites, then gently dip into the sesame seed mix. Place the salmon squares, sesame side up, on the baking sheet. The recipe can be prepared ahead to this point. Cover and refrigerate for up to 6 hours.

Bake salmon squares about 4–5 minutes, until just cooked through. Remove and insert a toothpick or skewer into each square. Serve warm or at room temperature with Lemon-Miso Sauce.

SERVES 12 AS AN APPETIZER

LEMON-MISO SAUCE

½ cup mayonnaise

3 tablespoons fresh lemon juice

2 tablespoons white miso

1 tablespoon mirin or sake

2 teaspoons lemon zest

1 teaspoon fresh ginger, minced

1 tablespoon chives, chopped

Black pepper, freshly ground, to taste

Stir all ingredients together in a small bowl until blended. Season with pepper to taste. Chill for at least an hour before serving.

MAKES ¾ CUP

Endive Spears with Herbed Goat Cheese, Edible Flowers, and Plum Salsa

I wanted to incorporate organic edible flowers into the menu for this party in the garden; I had used them often in salads, though never as part of an appetizer. In this dish, crisp Belgian endive spears are filled with a creamy herbed goat cheese and plum salsa, then topped with a single flower. The hors d'oeuvre definitely focused attention on the importance of preserving the delicate balance between humanity and our environment. With an increased interest in organic produce, edible flowers are now available at most supermarkets, but you can also use chive blossoms or mint sprigs.

3 heads Belgian endive

Herbed Goat Cheese (RECIPEA FOLLOWS)

Plum Salsa (RECIPEA FOLLOWS)

3 dozen organic edible flowers

Trim the bottoms from the endive spears and separate into individual spears. Spread one tablespoon of Herbed Goat Cheese along the bottom of each spear. (The endive can be prepared and refrigerated 6 hours ahead.) Next, spread a spoonful of Plum Salsa on top of the goat cheese, and gently press one edible flower on top. Serve immediately.

SERVES 12

HERBED GOAT CHEESE

1 11-ounce goat-cheese log, room temperature

¾ cup heavy cream

2 tablespoons fresh mint, finely chopped

2 tablespoons fresh cilantro, finely chopped

Salt and freshly ground pepper to taste

Combine first 4 ingredients in a large bowl. Using a handheld or stand mixer, mix on medium speed until well combined, about 1 minute. Season with salt and pepper. Refrigerate, covered, until ready to use, up to 3 days.

MAKES 1½ CUPS

PLUM SALSA

2 tablespoons olive oil

2 teaspoons sugar

1 tablespoon fresh lime juice

4 ripe red plums (such as Japanese Santa Rosa or Red Beaut), stoned and diced

1 medium Fuji apple, peeled and diced

1 small red onion, finely chopped

½ cup cilantro, chopped

¼ cup mint, chopped

Salt and freshly ground black pepper to taste

In a bowl, stir together the olive oil, sugar, and lime juice until the sugar is dissolved. Add the remaining ingredients and stir to combine. Season with salt and pepper. Allow the flavors to blend for 10 minutes. Serve at room temperature.

MAKES 5 CUPS

PORK MARINADE

¼ cup oyster sauce*

¼ cup soy sauce

1 tablespoon fresh ginger, chopped

3 garlic cloves, minced

2 teaspoons sugar

1 tablespoon rice vinegar

2 teaspoons Sriracha chili-garlic sauce*

¼ teaspoon red pepper flakes

In a medium bowl, mix the pork cubes with the marinade ingredients, tossing to coat well. Cover and refrigerate for at least 2 hours or overnight.

Each Inari pocket should be sealed on three of the four sides. Cut each piece in half so that one portion remains sealed on three sides; this pocket will hold the pork filling. (You can reserve the remaining halves for another use, such as soup or stir-fry.)

Drain the pork. Heat a wok over high heat and add 2 tablespoons of oil. When oil begins to shimmer, add the pork and stir fry, stirring constantly, until cooked through, about 4–5 minutes. Remove the pork and set aside.

Heat the remaining 2 tablespoons of oil in the wok over high heat. Add the garlic and ginger and stir until the garlic just begins to brown. Add the cabbage, scallions, bell pepper, and black pepper. Cook, stirring constantly, until the cabbage is tender, about 5 minutes. Reduce heat to medium.

Add the cooked pork and any remaining marinade. Sprinkle the cornstarch over the mixture and stir to combine. Cook until the sauce thickens and the pork is warmed through, about 5 minutes. Remove from heat.

To serve, fill each Inari pocket with a spoonful of warm pork and cabbage, leaving any excess liquid in the pan. If you desire, you can tie each Inari with a chive for garnish, and to hold the pockets together on the platter. Serve immediately.

*Inari pockets, oyster sauce, and Sriracha chili-garlic sauce can be found in specialty stores or the Asian section of many large supermarkets. You can also make steamed wontons with this flavorful filling.

MAKES 24 INARI POCKETS

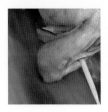

Chicken Yakitori Skewers

Much like American hot-dog stands, Japanese *yakitori-ya* stands serve a popular fast food. Rush-hour commuters often enjoy a cold beer with a few sweet pieces of grilled chicken and scallions before boarding their train home. Small red lanterns with the character for bird, or *tori*, identify these stands. Bite-sized morsels of chicken are skewered and grilled over fragrant charcoal fires, which infuse a distinctive, smoky flavor. Customers choose between a soy-based sauce (*tare*) or salt (*shio*) to flavor the meat. The cooked meat can be sprinkled with shichimi, a seven-spice seasoning that includes red chile flakes and sesame seeds and is a staple on most Japanese restaurant tables, much like our Tabasco sauce. For a quick Japanese-style dinner, serve *yakitori-don*—warmed chicken skewers over a bowl of rice.

1 cup sake

2 cups mirin

2 cups soy sauce

¼ cup sugar

¼ cup honey

2 tablespoons sesame oil

4 tablespoons sesame seeds

3 tablespoons cornstarch

24 8-inch bamboo skewers,
    soaked in water for 30 minutes

3 pounds boneless, skinless chicken thighs or breasts,
    cut into 1-inch cubes*

2 large green peppers, seeded, ribbed,
    and cut into 1-inch squares

4 bunches scallions, white part only,
    cut into 1-inch pieces

Vegetable oil spray

Shichimi seasoning or Thai chili-garlic sauce (optional)**

To make the glaze, combine the sake, mirin, soy sauce, sugar, honey, sesame oil, and sesame seeds in a small saucepan. Bring to a boil, reduce heat to medium, and simmer for about an hour, or until the mixture is thickened and reduced by half. You should have about 3 cups. Whisk in the cornstarch and bring the mixture back to a boil, stirring constantly. Remove from heat and cool to room temperature. Sauce can be made ahead and refrigerated, covered, for up to 3 days.

To prepare the yakitori, thread the soaked skewers with chicken, green pepper, and scallions, alternating the ingredients. Begin and end with the chicken pieces and leave about 3 inches of the wood exposed on each end. For appetizer-sized portions, use three pieces of chicken and two each of the peppers and scallions per skewer. Skewers can be made a day ahead, covered, and refrigerated.

To cook, preheat the grill to medium. Coat the grates with vegetable oil spray. Place the skewers in a large container. Reserve ½ cup of the glaze for a dipping sauce, and pour the remainder over the skewers. Using a brush, coat all sides of the yakitori with the glaze. Place skewers on the grill and cook, basting and turning frequently, until the meat and vegetables are cooked through and slightly charred, about 8–10 minutes. Serve warm or at room temperature with dipping sauce or shichimi.

To make the dipping sauce, mix the reserved glaze with ½ cup Thai chili-garlic sauce.

*Any lean meat can be substituted for the chicken; for an appetizing vegetarian alternative, use whole-button mushrooms with red or green peppers.

**Shichimi seasoning and Thai chili-garlic sauce, also known as Sriracha, can be found in specialty stores or the Asian section of many large supermarkets.

SERVES 12

Raspberry-Almond Tea Cakes

A classic combination of almond and raspberry renders Annie B's miniature cakes irresistible. Top each one with a candied violet or a fresh raspberry. You will need an instant-read thermometer that measures up to 120°F.

1 recipe Almond Pound Cake, baked in a 9x13-inch pan
½ cup Amaretto Simple Syrup (RECIPEA FOLLOWS)
¾ cup raspberry jam, with seeds
1 cup Amaretto Buttercream Frosting (RECIPEA FOLLOWS)
Candied violets or fresh raspberries, for garnish

TO ASSEMBLE THE CAKE

Using a sharp serrated knife, carefully cut the pound cake in half horizontally, so you have two 9x13-inch pieces. Place one half of the cake, cut side up, on a parchment-lined pan or tray. Using a pastry brush, distribute half the Amaretto Simple Syrup over the cake. Then spread the raspberry jam over that half, all the way to the edges. Top with the other cake layer, placing the cut side down. Brush with the remaining syrup. Chill until the syrup is absorbed, about 30 minutes. The cake can be made to this point and frozen for up to a month. Thaw before continuing.

TO MAKE THE TEA CAKES

Evenly spread a thin layer of Amaretto Buttercream Frosting over the top of the cake. You might not use all the frosting. If you wish, you can make a striped pattern in the frosting with a cake comb or a serrated knife. Refrigerate the cake until set, approximately 2 hours.

Using a sharp serrated knife, trim the sides of the cake so that you have a straight-sided rectangle with no frosting on the sides. Cut the cake into 36 1×2-inch pieces: 6 lengthwise 1-inch pieces and 6 widthwise 2-inch pieces. (You may get an extra row lengthwise, depending on how you trim your cake.) For easier cutting, rinse the knife in hot water and dry it between cuts.

Refrigerate the tea cakes until ready to serve, or up to 2 days. Top with candied violets or fresh raspberries just before serving.

ALMOND POUND CAKE

Makes 1 9x13-inch layer or 2 9-inch round layer cakes

    1 tablespoon shortening, for pan

    2 sticks unsalted butter, room temperature

    1 cup sugar

    ¼ teaspoon salt

    1 tablespoon almond extract

    4 large eggs

    ¼ cup whole milk

    2 cups cake flour

    ¾ teaspoon baking powder

Position a rack in the top half of the oven. Preheat to 325°F.

Grease the bottom and sides of a 9x13-inch baking pan or two 9-inch round cake pans with shortening. Line the bottom(s) with parchment or waxed paper. Set aside.

Using an electric or stand mixer, cream the butter, sugar, salt, and almond extract on medium speed until light and fluffy, about 5 minutes. In a small bowl, whisk one of the eggs and the milk until blended. Set aside. Sift together the flour and baking powder. Set aside.

When the butter mixture is light and fluffy, reduce the speed to low and add the remaining eggs, one at a time, scraping the bowl between additions. The batter may be lumpy. Alternate additions of flour and milk (mixing and scraping between each addition), beginning and ending with the flour mixture.

Pour the batter into the prepared pan(s) and spread evenly. Bake for 18–20 minutes, rotating pans halfway if using round pans. The cake will be pale on top but will spring back when touched lightly. Let cake cool in pan(s) for 10 minutes, then remove and cool completely on a wire rack before continuing. If desired, cover the cake in plastic wrap and refrigerate overnight.

MAKES APPROXIMATELY 36 TEA CAKES

AMARETTO SIMPLE SYRUP

    ¼ cup sugar

    ¼ cup water

    2 tablespoons amaretto or other almond liqueur

Bring the sugar and water to a boil in a small saucepan. When the sugar has dissolved, add the liqueur and stir to combine. Cool before using. Syrup can be refrigerated for up to 2 weeks.

MAKES ABOUT ½ CUP

AMARETTO BUTTERCREAM FROSTING

This is a versatile recipe that can be varied by simply changing the flavoring. Experiment with other liqueurs, such as Grand Marnier or Crème de Cassis. Just remember that some liqueurs, such as Crème de Cassis, will change the color of the buttercream.

1 cup egg whites, from 6–7 large eggs

2½ cups sugar

4 sticks unsalted butter, room temperature

¼ cup amaretto or other almond liqueur

In the metal bowl of a stand mixer, combine the egg whites and sugar. Create a double boiler by placing the bowl over a saucepan half full of simmering water, so that the bottom of the bowl is just above the water. Stir the mixture constantly with a heat-proof rubber utensil until it measures 120°F on a thermometer. Immediately remove from heat.

Return the bowl to the stand mixer. Using the whip attachment, whip on high speed until stiff peaks form and the bottom of the bowl feels cool to the touch, about 15 minutes. (At this point, you shouldn't feel any sugar granules when you rub a small dab of the mixture between your thumb and forefinger.)

Reduce the mixer speed to medium. Add the butter slowly, tablespoon by tablespoon, making sure each addition is thoroughly mixed in. At some points, the mixture may look broken or unusable, but continue beating—it will pull together! When the butter is completely incorporated, add the liqueur. Continue to beat on medium speed for 2 minutes, then reduce the speed to low and beat for 2 additional minutes.

Refrigerate the buttercream in an airtight container for 2 weeks, or freeze for up to 3 months. Return to room temperature and beat again before using.

MAKES ABOUT 6 CUPS

Vicki's Oatmeal-Lemon Delicate Delights

This recipe came courtesy of Annie B's friend Vicki Helgenberg. The oatmeal gives the cookies an almost ethereal airiness and a distinctive crunch. You can enhance Vicki's recipe with other citrus zests, such as orange, lime, or grapefruit, or ¼ cup of a favorite chopped nut or dried fruit.

1 cup flour

½ teaspoon baking soda

¼ teaspoon salt

2 sticks unsalted butter, room temperature

1 cup sugar

2 teaspoons lemon extract

2 teaspoons lemon zest

1½ cups old-fashioned rolled oats

¼ cup nuts or dried fruit, chopped (optional)

Preheat oven to 350°F.

In a small bowl, whisk together the flour, baking soda, and salt. Set aside.

Using an electric or stand mixer, combine the butter and sugar. Beat on medium speed until light and fluffy, approximately 10 minutes, scraping down the sides of the bowl as needed. Beat in the lemon extract and lemon zest. Reduce the speed to low and stir in the flour mixture until just blended. With a spoon, stir in the rolled oats and nuts or dried fruit, if using, until well blended. The dough will be soft.

Drop by rounded spoonfuls 2 inches apart onto an ungreased baking sheet. Bake until lightly golden, about 13–15 minutes, rotating sheets halfway through to ensure even browning. Cool for 1 minute on the baking sheet, then remove to a wire rack and cool completely. Cookies can be stored in an airtight container for up to a week, or wrapped well and frozen for up to 2 months.

MAKES 4 DOZEN COOKIES

Grilled Tuna Niçoise Salad

The key to the delicate taste of this Provençal salad is the use of a mild French olive oil. For the traditional taste of Provence, Boston lettuce leaves, new potatoes, crisp haricots verts, teardrop tomatoes, and brine-cured niçoise olives are topped with sushi-grade rare grilled tuna. A generous drizzle of olive oil and fresh lemon juice finishes the dish. Golden- and green-hued unfiltered olive oils from the South of France are almost buttery in taste, with herbal overtones. They are a perfect pairing for grilled fish and fresh vegetables. Look for Nicolas Alziari or A l'Olivier olive oil from Nice.

2 pounds small Yukon Gold potatoes, quartered

2 tablespoons French extra virgin olive oil,
 plus about 1 cup for dressing

1 tablespoon lemon juice

Salt and freshly ground pepper to taste

2 pounds slender green beans,
 such as haricots verts, trimmed

Vegetable oil spray

2 pounds sushi-grade tuna, about 1 inch thick

¼ cup olive oil

4 heads Boston lettuce leaves, separated

2 pints teardrop or grape tomatoes, halved

6 hard-cooked eggs, quartered*

1 cup niçoise olives, pitted

½ cup capers, drained

2 lemons, cut into 6 wedges each

Place potatoes in a medium saucepan and add enough cold water to cover. Bring to a boil and cook until tender when pierced with a fork, about 7–8 minutes. Drain and place in a large bowl. Toss with the olive oil and lemon juice. Season with salt and pepper. Cool to room temperature.

Cook the green beans in a pot of boiling salted water until crisp-tender, about 3 minutes. Drain and submerge in a bowl of ice water. Drain again and set aside to dry.

Preheat closed grill on high for 10 minutes. Reduce heat to medium. Lightly spray the grates with vegetable oil to prevent sticking. Brush the tuna with olive oil and season with salt and pepper. Grill the tuna, turning once, until cooked on the outside but still pink inside, about 3–4 minutes per side. Remove from heat and let rest for 5 minutes. Cut into ½-inch-thick slices. (Tuna can also be cooked in a lightly oiled grill pan or broiled for about 3–4 minutes per side for medium.)

Arrange the lettuce leaves on a large serving platter and top with potato quarters, green beans, tomatoes, hard-cooked eggs, and olives. Arrange the tuna slices over the salad and scatter capers on top. Lightly drizzle with olive oil and season with salt and pepper. Serve at room temperature with lemon wedges.

*To hard-cook eggs: Place eggs in a medium saucepan. Add enough cold water to cover. Bring the water to a boil, remove the pan from heat, cover, and let sit for 15 minutes. Drain the eggs and rinse under cold water until cool. Peel immediately.

SERVES 12

CHAPTER EIGHT *drumthwacket*

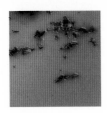

Creamy Tomato and Carrot Soup

I like to serve this soup in the summer, chilled and garnished with fresh herbs, but it's always welcome warm during our snowy New Jersey winters. The apple, tomato, and lemon combination is refreshing and light, and the curry imparts a hint of spiciness. If you prefer a lighter version, you can omit the heavy cream or use light cream. It's delicious either way.

A bouquet garni, or broth posy, is a fantastic way to lend deep flavor to soups and stews. Herbs—traditionally, a trio of bay leaf, parsley, and thyme—are tied together in a small piece of cheesecloth with kitchen string and simmered in the liquid along with the other ingredients. The spices in our bouquet garni add a distinctive flavor.

¼ cup unsalted butter

1 tablespoon olive oil

1 medium onion, chopped

¾ pound (about 2½ cups) carrots, peeled and chopped

1 Granny Smith apple, peeled and chopped

2 cloves garlic, minced

1 tablespoon light brown sugar

2½ pounds (about 4 cups) tomatoes, peeled and chopped

4 cups chicken stock

1 tablespoon fresh lemon juice

1 teaspoon fresh lemon zest, plus more for garnish, if desired

1 teaspoon curry powder

1 bouquet garni (10 peppercorns, 4 cloves,
    4 allspice berries, 2 bay leaves, and 2 thyme sprigs)

1 cup heavy cream, plus ½ cup for whipping if serving soup cold

Salt and freshly ground pepper to taste

Fresh parsley for garnish

Melt the butter and olive oil in a heavy soup pot over medium heat. Add the onion and cook until soft and translucent, stirring occasionally, about 10 minutes. Add the carrots, apple, and garlic. Cook, stirring frequently, until softened and just beginning to color, about 8–10 minutes. Stir in the brown sugar and cook another 2 minutes. Add the tomatoes, stock, lemon juice, lemon zest, curry powder, and bouquet garni. Bring to a simmer, reduce heat to low, cover, and cook until thickened, about 45 minutes.

Discard the bouquet garni. Puree the soup in small batches in a food processor or food mill until almost smooth but with a little texture remaining. Transfer the soup to a saucepan and add the cup of heavy cream. Rewarm over low heat. Season with salt and pepper. Soup may be served warm or chilled.

To serve chilled, puree the soup mixture and refrigerate for 2 hours. Thin with a little stock, if necessary. Whip the remaining heavy cream to soft peaks, and top each serving with a few tablespoons. Garnish with fresh parsley and lemon zest.

*You can substitute 1 28-ounce can plus 1 14-ounce can peeled whole tomatoes, if desired.

MAKES 2 QUARTS

Jack's Lobster Salad

Texas Chocolate Cake

Lobster is one of those ingredients that instantly make guests feel special. Served on a bun, lobster salad can be perfectly casual, but it can also exude elegance, as when served on a small bed of greens. Regardless, it is always a luxury item, so it was our choice for a luncheon at the Governor's Mansion. Jack Morrison of Nassau Street Seafood shared his recipe for one of the store's most popular take-out salads. This is an incredibly rich dish; small servings will suffice. Garnish each plate with endive spears, a touch of tiny champagne grapes, and an edible flower for a stunning and luscious salad.

2 pounds cooked lobster meat (tails and claws), coarsely chopped

1 tablespoon lemon juice, freshly squeezed

3 tablespoons mayonnaise, or to taste

¼ cup diced celery

1 tablespoon capers

White pepper to taste

Combine all ingredients in a large bowl, and mix gently until combined. Serve immediately or chill, covered, until ready to serve, up to 24 hours.

MAKES 5 CUPS

Along with her coconut cake topped with mounds of fluffy seven-minute icing, this is the cake my brothers and I begged our mother to make when we were kids. When I was in elementary school, she brought the cake to a school event, and the head of our school cafeteria asked for the recipe. Little did my mother know that this small act of kindness would forever change the way the children looked at cafeteria food. Throughout my entire public school education in Fort Worth, Texas, this chocolate cake, called Sheath Cake on the menu, was served every Friday on our school lunch trays.

Years later, when I realized that just about everyone else's mother in Texas had the recipe, I decided to research the source. During pioneer days, it was called funeral cake. A buttermilk-based cake, it stays moist for at least a week and could survive a long wagon ride to a distant relative's funeral. I decided to rename it Texas Chocolate Cake in honor of my home state. While this cake has down-home roots, I think it's the ultimate chocolate cake. I'm sure that at some point, Agnes Taylor Pyne must have enjoyed a slice of this baking tradition at someone's home in Flower Mound. I think she would have liked that it was served in her grandparents' outdoor dining room in Princeton. This recipe is dedicated to my mother and Agnes.

2 sticks margarine

4 tablespoons cocoa powder

1 cup water

2 cups all-purpose flour

2 cups sugar

1 teaspoon baking soda

1 teaspoon cinnamon

2 eggs

½ cup buttermilk

1 teaspoon vanilla extract

Chocolate Icing (RECIPEA FOLLOWS)

Preheat oven to 400°F.

Grease and flour the bottom and sides of a 9×13-inch Pyrex cake pan and set aside.

In a small saucepan over low heat, melt the margarine, cocoa, and water. Stir to mix and set aside to cool.

Sift the flour, sugar, baking soda, and cinnamon into a large mixing bowl. Add the eggs, buttermilk, vanilla, and cooled margarine mixture. Beat on low until blended.

Pour the batter into the prepared pan. Bake for 20 minutes, or until a toothpick inserted in the center comes out clean and the top springs back when touched. Cool the cake for 5 minutes on a wire rack, then pour Chocolate Icing over the top, distributing evenly with a knife. Cake should still be warm when you ice. Cool completely before serving.

CHOCOLATE ICING

1 stick margarine

4 tablespoons cocoa powder

6 tablespoons milk

1 1-pound box confectioners' sugar

1 teaspoon vanilla extract

1 cup chopped pecans, optional

In a small saucepan over low heat, melt the margarine together with the cocoa powder and milk. Whisk to blend.

Sift the confectioners' sugar into the bowl of a stand mixer. Add the margarine mixture and beat on low until the sugar is incorporated. Add the vanilla extract and beat on high until the icing is smooth and glossy. Stir in the pecans, if using. Immediately pour over warm cake.

MAKES 1 9×13-INCH CAKE

Mum's Sippin' Whiskey

I was delighted when Daphne Townsend, former executive director of the Drumthwacket Foundation, told me she had one of Agnes Taylor Pyne's recipes. When she recited it to me, I had to laugh: It was not at all what I had expected. I could just imagine Agnes sitting in the garden with her husband, Larry, sipping this drink over ice on a hot summer evening at their farm in Flower Mound, Texas. Somehow, Agnes, who was descended from a signer of the Declaration of Independence and grew up on an estate close to my present Princeton home, ended up owning a farm near my hometown of Fort Worth, Texas. I like to think this might prove the old saying "If you weren't born a Texan, get there as fast as you can!"

Rock candy was used originally by pharmacists to make medicines for many kinds of illnesses. It is one of the oldest and purest forms of candy. While we didn't have a year to age the sugar and bourbon, the recipe has the ingredients for a good strong Southern drink, the kind you feel only when you stand up. The concoction could probably cure just about any ailment, so imbibe gently—there's a reason it's called . . .

MUM'S SIPPIN' WHISKEY

Rock candy, the kind with a string running through*
1 pint good-quality bourbon

Fill a crystal decanter with chunks of rock candy and pour the bourbon over.

Seal tightly and let sit until the sugar has dissolved and only the string remains. Strain and age for at least 1 month, or preferably 1 year.

Keeps indefinitely.

*Daphne uses rock candy from Hansel & Gretel in Carmel, California, but any good rock candy will do. Buy the large chunks. Or, for great fun, make your own with your kids. It's a simple but tasty science experiment.

MAKES 1 PINT

recipea index

resources

ricardo barros *principal photographer*

RICARDO BARROS is a professional photographer based in Morrisville, Pennsylvania. He is a versatile craftsman comfortable with both studio and location work, and his clients include: US Airways, Seagram's Americas, Princeton University, and Grounds For Sculpture, where he has been the principal photographer since the park's inception. Barros' own works are included in the permanent collections of the Smithsonian American Art Museum; the Philadelphia Museum of Art; Harvard University's Fogg Art Museum; the DeCordova Museum; Grounds For Sculpture; the New Jersey State Museum; the Museum of Art of São Paulo, in Brazil; and the Museum of Image and Sound, also in Brazil. Barros is represented by Marsha Child Contemporary Gallery, in Princeton, New Jersey. Barros created Image Spring Press and produced its first title, *Facing Sculpture: A Portfolio of Portraits, Sculpture and Related Ideas*, in 2004. He can be reached through his website, www.ricardobarros.com.

Vladimir Kanevsky with New York Skyline, 1998.

262

music

LAURIE ALTMAN
Westminster Conservatory
Princeton, New Jersey
(609) 921-7104
www.rider.edu/westminster

MASAYI ISHIGURE
Japanese Koto and Shamisen
masayo-koto.home.att.net

artists

FAY SCIARRA
Lawrenceville, New Jersey
(609) 844-0879
www.faysciarra.com

MARSHA CHILD CONTEMPORARY
Princeton, New Jersey
(609) 497-7330
www.mchildcontemporary.com

SHELLEY ROE
Roe's Petals
Princeton, New Jersey
(609) 497-0380
www.roespetals.com

renovate / redesign

RONALD BERLIN
Princeton, New Jersey
(609) 921-1800
www.ronaldberlin.com

**BRAHANEY ARCHITECTURAL
   ASSOCIATES**
Rocky Hill, New Jersey
(609) 497-9337
www.brahaney.com

GLEN FRIES ASSOCIATES
Princeton, New Jersey
(609) 924-8700

KOCH & WEBBER ARCHITECTS
Earlysville, Virginia
434-973-8470

LASLEY CONSTRUCTION
Rocky Hill, New Jersey
(609) 921-2822
www.lasleyconstruction.com

RALPH LERNER, ARCHITECT PC
Princeton, New Jersey
(609) 683-1001
www.rlapc.net

MICHAEL GRAVES & ASSOCIATES
Princeton, New Jersey
(609) 924-6409
www.michaelgraves.com

featured organizations and groups

ARTS COUNCIL OF PRINCETON
Princeton, New Jersey
(609) 924-8777
www.artscouncilofprinceton.org

BATTLEFIELD STATE PARK
Princeton, New Jersey
(609) 921-0074
www.state.nj.us/dep/parksandforests
www.10CrucialDays.org

**CHILDREN'S HEALTH
   ENVIRONMENTAL COALITION**
Princeton, New Jersey
(609) 252-1915
Los Angeles, California
(310) 652-2901
www.checnet.org

**DELAWARE AND RARITAN CANAL
   STATE PARK**
Somerset, New Jersey
www.dandrcanal.com

DRUMTHWACKET FOUNDATION
Princeton, New Jersey
(609) 683-0057
www.drumthwacket.org

NEW JERSEY SYMPHONY ORCHESTRA
www.njsymphony.org

MORVEN
Princeton, New Jersey
(609) 924-8144
www.historicmorven.org

PRINCETON SYMPHONY ORCHESTRA
www.princetonsymphony.org

research assistance

HARVEY S. FIRESTONE LIBRARY
University Archives
Department of Rare Books
and Special Collections
Princeton University Library
Princeton, New Jersey
(609) 258-3242
http://libweb.princeton.edu

HISTORICAL SOCIETY OF PRINCETON
Princeton, New Jersey
(609) 921-6748
www.princetonhistory.org

LIBRARY OF CONGRESS
Prints and Photographs Division
Historic American Buildings Survey
Washington, D.C.
(202) 707-5640
www.loc.gov

SEELEY G. MUDD MANUSCRIPT LIBRARY
Princeton, New Jersey
(609) 258-6345
www.princeton.edu/mudd

SMITHSONIAN INSTITUTION
Washington, D.C.
(202) 633-1000
www.smithsonian.org

shopping

ASHTON WHYTE
Pennington, New Jersey
(609) 737-7171
www.ashtonwhyte.com

FRAN JAY
Depression Glass Dealer
Lambertville, New Jersey
(609) 397-1571
glasjay@erols.com

GASIOR'S FURNITURE
Belle Mead, New Jersey
(908) 874-8383
www.gasiorsfurniture.com

GO FOR BAROQUE, INC.
Princeton, New Jersey
(609) 497-3500
www.goforbaroque.com

GRAVES DESIGN STUDIO STORES
Princeton, New Jersey
(800) 279-2642
www.michaelgraves.com

HAMILTON JEWELERS
Princeton, New Jersey
(609) 683-4200
www.hamiltonjewelers.com

ed batejan *chef*

ann bartholomay *baker*

Ed has been a professional chef for sixteen years, working in the Princeton and Bucks County areas. Ed's love of cooking developed early on from watching his father prepare gourmet meals for the family. Ed has cooked for the former president and vice president of the United States, the former governor of New Jersey, senior officials of the United Nations, and many top corporate officials. He currently works for an off-premise catering company and specializes in private catering. In his downtime (yeah, right, downtime for a chef!), Ed enjoys teaching the future of the culinary world, his three young children, to cook.

Ann Bartholomay, a graduate of the Culinary Institute of America, was the first female executive chef for Omni Hotels of America. She founded Annie B's Confections in Bucks County, Pennsylvania, in 1986 and became known for her artistic wedding cakes filled with rich gourmet flavors. Her fine line of artisan-baked products has since expanded to include an endless array of individual desserts, miniature pastries, sliced cakes, tarts, pies, cupcakes, and cookies.

credits

marek bulaj *photographer*

Marek Bulaj has worked as a staff photographer for world-renowned architect Michael Graves & Associates for the past twelve years. Previously, he was a freelance photographer for the *New York Daily News* and staff photographer at *Jasna Polana*, the private estate of Barbara Piasecka Johnson, in Princeton, New Jersey.

Marek's photographs have appeared in exhibition catalogs such as *Opus Sacrum* (Warsaw, 1990, and Liechtenstein, 1991) and *Drawings by Raphael and His Circle* (the Pierpont Morgan Library, 1987), and in many publications, including *The New York Times, Art & Antiques, New Jersey Monthly, Paris Match, Hello!, ¡Hola!, Gioto, Stone World,* and *Carrousel.* Marek studied at the International Center of Photography in New York and at New York University's Tisch School of Arts.

MACKENZIE-CHILDS, INC.
www.mackenzie-childs.com

MICAWBER BOOKS
Princeton, New Jersey
(609) 921-8454
www.micawber.com

MOTTAHEDEH & CO., INC.
New York, NY
(800) 242-3050
www.mottahedeh.com

OLD CHARLESTON
   JOGGLING BOARD COMPANY
Charleston, South Carolina
(843) 723-4331
www.oldcharlestonjogglingboard.com

PINS AND NEEDLES
Princeton, New Jersey
(609) 921-9075
www.pinsandneedles.biz

PRINCETON UNIVERSITY BOOKSTORE
Princeton, New Jersey
(609) 921-8500
www.pustore.com

RUBY PEARL CLOTHING
www.rubypearl.com

SIMON PEARCE
Princeton, New Jersey
(609) 279-0444
www.simonpearce.com

THE WINGED PIG
Princeton, New Jersey
(609) 924-1212
www.thewingedpigonline.com

dining

BENT SPOON
Princeton, New Jersey
(609) 924-BENT
thebentspoon@verizon.net

BLUE POINT GRILL
Princeton, New Jersey
(609) 921-1211
www.bluepointgrill.com

CONTE'S PIZZA
Princeton, New Jersey
(609) 921-8041

HALO PUB
Princeton, New Jersey
(609) 921-1710

HOAGIE HAVEN
Princeton, New Jersey
(609) 921-7723

MAIN STREET EURO-AMERICAN
   BISTRO & BAR
Princeton, New Jersey
(609) 921-2779
www.mainstreetprinceton.com

MAIN STREET HOMETOWN BAKERY
   & COFFEEHOUSE
Kingston, New Jersey
(609) 921-2778
www.mainstreetprinceton.com

MEDITERRA
Princeton, New Jersey
(609) 252-9680
www.t2restaurants.com

MOONDOGGIE CAFÉ
Princeton, New Jersey
(609) 252-0300

NASSAU BAGEL & SUSHI
Princeton, New Jersey
(609) 497-3275

NASSAU STREET SEAFOOD
   AND PRODUCE COMPANY
Princeton, New Jersey
(609) 921-0620

PIZZA STAR
Princeton, New Jersey
(609) 921-7422

PJ'S PANCAKE HOUSE
Princeton, New Jersey
(609) 924-1353
www.pancakes.com

SMALL WORLD COFFEE
Princeton, New Jersey
(609) 924-4377
www.smallworldcoffee.com

A TASTE OF MEXICO
Princeton, New Jersey
(609) 252-1575

TERESA'S CAFÉ ITALIANO
Princeton, New Jersey
(609) 921-1974
www.t2restaurants.com

THOMAS SWEET ICE CREAM
   & CHOCOLATES
Princeton, New Jersey
(609) 924-7222
www.thomassweet.com

TORTUGA'S MEXICAN VILLAGE
Princeton, New Jersey
(609) 924-5143

TRIUMPH BREWING COMPANY
Princeton, New Jersey
(609) 924-7855
www.triumphbrewing.com

VICTOR'S PIZZERIA
Princeton, New Jersey
(609) 924-5515

WITHERSPOON BREAD COMPANY
Princeton, New Jersey
(609) 688-0188
www.t2restaurants.com

YANKEE DOODLE TAP ROOM
Princeton, New Jersey
(609) 921-7500
www.nassauinn.com

DID SOMEONE SAY COOKIE ? ! ? ! ? !

three more dishes ...

deborah tunnell *the queen*

Born in Fort Worth, Texas, Debbie Tunnell baked her first cake for her grandfather's eightieth birthday and has been enchanted by the art of the kitchen ever since. Her love of good food and relaxed entertaining led her to seek out a career in catering, party planning, and recipe testing and development. She jointly founded Recipeas4u LLC, in 2001 and began the four-year-journey to what would eventually become her first book, *Sacred Spaces: Princeton Parties, Gatherings and Celebrations.* She is a member of the International Association of Culinary Professionals and the American Institute of Wine & Food and has a BA in Marketing and Communications.

dale engelbert *the in-between*

A native New Jerseyan who spent many formative years in North Carolina, Dale Engelbert left the beach and now finds herself back in New Jersey. Cofounder of Recipeas4u LLC, she worked as a sales and marketing consultant for the gourmet food industry before forming the Princeton Media Group, a multimedia design company, in 1999. Dale studied at the School of Visual Arts and is a graduate and member of the alumni board of East Carolina University. She sets an eye-catching table and has mastered the art of napkin folding.

susan szymanski *the princess*

A former graphic designer for Michael Graves & Associates, Susan Szymanski formed her own company, Moonlight Design, in 2001. This full-service design studio focuses a passion for paper on event-related graphics and social stationery. Susan holds a BFA in illustration from Moore College of Art and Design and has pursued botanical illustration through the New York Botanical Garden. This Jersey girl loves to bake exquisite holiday cookies and has an enviable collection of whimsical 1940s table linens.